PARENTING IN THE AGE *of* PERFECTION

A Modern Guide to Nurturing a Success Mindset

CANDICE LAPIN

For my late father, my personal coach whose voice I heard as I wrote this whole book.

CONTENTS:

*Names throughout this book have been changed
to protect the identity of youth.*

Parent:

"a father or mother"
"a caregiver of offspring"
- Dictionary.com

ACKNOWLEDGEMENTS

I am deeply grateful to all of the people who have contributed and supported me in the completion of this book. I want to especially thank Stephanie Dunn for her early edits on the initial draft. I want to thank Marissa Dowd for helping me carve out time in the early inception of this book. I would also like to thank Annie Kee for helping take so much off my plate so that I could put my full focus on this grand opus!

This book also would not have been possible without the contribution of my incredible team of managers, coaches and tutors. I am so lucky to have found in all of you such kindred spirits who are as dedicated to growth and transformation as I am! You all have inspired me to take our stories to the streets and to parents everywhere.

I want to finally thank my family: Mom, Jason, Tippy, Celina, Gaby, Steve, Laura, Anna, Bob and Joseph.

PREFACE

I would like to start by qualifying and saying I never thought I would end up in education. Although, I am sure many people start their books out saying they were the unlikeliest person in their field. But, I am the most unlikely teacher. I never gave teaching or education as a life path that much thought. It wasn't in the cards. I was a very A-type personality. Teaching seemed more laid back. I was in the fast lane. I worked in Hollywood, then law for a now Fortune 500 tech company, then a fashion designer, and finally a startup doyenne. I was the girl who seemed on the fast track if I could make up my mind for goodness sakes.

I ended up working with children in the unlikeliest of circumstances. It was 2008. I was one of the few entrepreneurs who thought it was a good idea to start a business that year. Anderson Cooper had pretty much declared the end of the economy, but I thought I could prove everyone wrong. It was the perfect year to raise money because no one else would be doing it! I guess a few others had the same idea because I was invited to join an incubator with a class size of about 8 companies. Needless to say, the business went for a few years but never took off. Go figure—difficult-to-impossible economy.

By the end of 2010, I was looking for an outlet. I wanted something to distract me from the heartlessness of what I was doing. I wanted something more fulfilling than pitching

Venture Capitalists for money for a startup that I no longer believed in. That outlet proved life altering. I didn't know it at the time. I got a little job tutoring two fifth graders. Two very shy and very sweet young elementary age students. It was fabulous. I was in it for the pure joy. Those were the early days.

Before I knew it, I had thrown in the towel on my startup. My parents were beside themselves. How could their very smart, Ivy League educated daughter give up a six-figure salary for a tutoring gig? You could feel the cringe as the thought crossed their minds. I didn't give them a choice. It was more like, "Mom, Dad, this is happening." My father and mother were worried. How would I survive? What would they tell their friends?

Let me tell you that there were more than a few puzzled looks on clients' faces, as the door would open. What was a 34-year-old former attorney in designer clothing doing tutoring? Wasn't this an utter waste of my time? I even had a few mothers try to set me up on other job interviews as they were convinced that I was wasting my valuable skills. But, was I?

I had no idea the sort of issues in education I had stumbled upon. No one was actively talking about the problems I saw. I will admit that for a couple of years, I stayed relatively quiet. I was, after all, an outsider. I didn't have a Master's in Education. I certainly wasn't a psychologist or a neuropsychologist giving diagnoses. I didn't get my Educational Therapy degree as my godmother had so asked.

Who had the time? I didn't. As my business expanded, I started to notice the issues that I hope to help heal in this book.

You have heard the debate on nature versus nurture. In my office, I believe that students no matter their "wiring" can be "nurtured" to be good—if not, great—students and successful people. Those bad behaviors and those learning challenges your child faces can all be molded, shaped for the better and turned around well before that time. If you are coming to this book and your child is 14—good news, you have time. If you are coming to this book and your child is 16—you're still good. If your child is 9, even better, we have a longer runway to make some changes. Their behaviors, performance in school, and confidence are capable of being rewired for the better!

NOTE TO EDUCATORS

This book might be a fun read for you. This is not a technical book on educational theories. Nor is this book a technical argument against the merits of John Dewey's processes or his ideology or the incredible progressive thought that he spawned. This is not a critique of the Waldorf program or the Montessori schools. I truly respect the thought coming out of these schools. We need children to be responsible respectful citizens of the world and these schools of thought are all critical to creating that.

INTRODUCTION

If there was one take-away from the Varsity Blues Cheating scandal, it is that parents and kids today are in a real crisis. Parents are not just helicoptering anymore. They are bulldozing their children's way through life. These bulldozers don't feel comfortable letting their kids' lives play out. They have to intercede. They have to get involved to make certain that everything is going to be okay. They have to control the outcome. They, above all else, must protect their child. The Varsity Blues Cheating Scandal is an extreme of what has been going on for years. Parents are doing "too much." If the parents in the Varsity Blues Scandal could have taken the tests for their kids, they would have. This scandal brought to light the most damaging version of that impulse.

Underneath all that competition, we—parents, educators, and kids—have become a culture wildly afraid of imperfection. As an educator, I see this displayed as helicopter parenting and over-parenting. In our insta-everything world, all we want to do is show everyone what we think they want to see. We have become obsessed with not letting people see how imperfect we—*and our kids*—are. We pose. We curate. We give people our "good side."

Instead of criticizing what appears to be outrageous "displays of wealth" and "hubris" and "laziness" in that cheating scandal, I think we should embrace this moment as an opportunity to look at the root of these issues: fear of imperfection, fear of failure, and fear that our kids are not good enough.

Parents today know that something is amiss. To be honest, we all are worried. There is a myriad of issues that are running out of control. Kids can swipe right yet struggle to read. Videos are replacing teachers because kids don't have the "attention span" to listen to a real teacher anymore! Times tables and phonics lessons are being traded in for group projects and fad mathematics.[1] It's getting harder to get our children to focus, to start tasks and to finish just about anything. If they do finish, it is with the help of a parent or an adult. No one teaches kids how to learn! But the problem is deeper—kids today don't have resilience. Young kids and teens can't seem to take the reins of life anymore. When parents do too much for their kids, kids can't do for themselves. Now, troves of articles are dedicated to the problem of "Millennials" out in the workforce who lack life skills, *stick-to-itiveness* and resilience. Since the Varsity Blues scandal broke, it seems that everyone finally recognizes there is a problem, but where is anyone with a solution for parents?

Welcome to what I call the Perfection Age. In 2016, Mike Wadhera in TechCrunch had declared the death of the Information Age, an era characterized by telling people about yourself.[2] Think Facebook status updates and Twitter feeds. Remember those days, way back in 2016, when we used to tell people what we thought and what we were up to in 140 characters or less?[3] He singlehandedly declared the dawn of the "Experience Age" in which people favored showing people who they were on social media sites like Instagram and Snapchat.[4] Now, we didn't have to bother wasting time telling people anything; we could show them through a stream of picture updates!

But forget the Experience Age. We have zoomed way past that. I would argue that we are now in an "uber curated" Perfection Age, where you are no longer showing people who you are. An Instagram page is no longer an extension of a Facebook page with pictured memories but rather a distinctly curated hyper-real version of who you are. Instead of posting the first photo taken, kids, teens and adults are stylizing their experiences as if they are on a professional fashion shoot. They must take the perfect photo in the perfect outfit. They must write the perfect hashtags. It is no longer enough to have your friends following you. Popularity is measured on a global scale. The concern is not winning homecoming princess or queen. Kids want to grow vast followings based on likes rather than genuine in real life exchanges. In a world like this, kids, teens, and parents are under far more pressure to appear perfect. That pressure for surface appearances is creating a host of new issues to resolve.

Issue #1: My child is going to school but doesn't know how to study

Around the spring of 2015, I started to notice a recurring pattern in this new age. Many parents were coming to me frustrated. They were annoyed that their child's school had taught them times tables or writing, but their child wasn't picking it up fast enough. Many parents lamented. How many times would their child need to be taught something for it to stick? Their children were learning information but it just wasn't sticking or happening fast enough!

Issue #2: The unstructured learning environment

Another problem brewing in the Perfection Age is the trendy "unstructured" and "inquiry-based" schooling. It looks good on the surface until you dig a little deeper and realize your child might not be getting a proper education. Many of these "current" and "progressive" schools have done away with teaching the very information that is necessary for a child to succeed in life. They have absolutely done away with tests, assessments, a curriculum, and above all else, *structure* in favor of inquiry-based learning. Students are allowed to pursue whatever peaks their interest. What sounded like a utopian experience free of the competition and the frustration we all dealt with in school has now turned 7th grade into a nightmare. Your child can't complete homework or projects without feeling overwhelmed because they didn't ease into homework over time. Now they have to catch up. You realize they have never read a book for comprehension. They have never learned their multiplication tables, so they are still counting on their fingers. You're panicked! You ask yourself—how on earth is my child going to move into high school, let alone the workforce?

Issue #3: The unstructured home

The third issue that impacts parents is establishing routines at home. A lot of parents absolutely don't want to set rules at home for fear of confrontation or even being *disliked*. Parents don't want their friends to think they are "bad parents" or have a "problem child." There are no bedtimes, no dinner times, and no homework times. Out of a need to create the "perfect" childhood for your children, kids are allowed to do what they want when they want. And, they never have to do anything they *don't* want to do. But, kids need the structure at home to remind them to eat when they are hungry and to go to bed, so they aren't grumpy in the morning. Otherwise, the next day is shot. They must be taught the skill of applying themselves to things they don't want to do. When they don't have structure, homework doesn't get completed on time and kids don't go to bed on time. Let's stop the pattern before it becomes a runaway train of hungry, angry, lonely and tired!

Issue #4: Technology and distractions

The fourth problem that seems to elude parents is technology and distractions. With all of that posing, curating, DMing and texting, kids today aren't reading and learning the way they used to. They are distracted. I often get an initial call from a parent that homework is taking their child well over 4 to 5 hours to complete. They are worried that the school is assigning too much homework. I will then arrive in homes to observe that this same child is doing homework with the TV on in the background, notifications pinging on their computer and a phone next to that computer—all away from the prying eyes of their parents. It isn't the school or homework. Children aren't able to put their full focus on homework. How on earth is anyone, let alone a young teenager supposed to complete anything with that level of distraction? No wonder our kids don't remember what they are reading. Or parents feel that their kids have focus issues. Their brains are being trained for constant interruption and distraction.

Issue #5: Avoidance

We come full circle to the helicopter parenting issue, the issue that prompted this guide. I observe many parents that are over-involved and kids who are equally *avoidant*. These young tweens and teens are mistaken: the gift of life is building the courage to face your obstacles head on. Instead, they speed through life trying to avoid confrontation and discomfort. They avoid office hours with teachers. They ignore their authority figures or coaches after something has gone awry in the hopes that they can avoid that feeling of disappointment. They then look to their parents to advocate for them. Those same parents go into a school or gym or dance company, guns blazing. Hoping to curate the perfect childhood, parents have started to do everything for their kids, including fight their battles. You know—the helicopter parent or the bulldozer! Although you might dread it, your teen's moments of discomfort are their opportunities for growth. Deciding to face a teacher after a bad grade is monumental! It's critical they learn how to spring back from failure and rebuild that confidence. It's important to learn how to navigate our conflicts; otherwise our lives become very small.

Issue #6: My child has trouble finishing a task or turning in homework.

Ah…*attention failure*, or the failure to maintain attention on any one task. The newest dis-*ease* of the Perfection Age. People—kids, teens and adults—are so addicted to their devices they don't stay focused on any single task. They "need" to switch. They can't finish an assignment without switching to look something up online that is unrelated. They are so used to having a TV, a watch, and an iPhone all grabbing for their attention, that doing reading for homework seems boring.

More and more kids are landing on my doorstep, not with classic ADD or ADHD, but rather with executive functioning issues and attention failure. Children that experience these issues might understand what steps are to be taken, but have difficulty sticking to the steps. They have trouble moving from one phase of a project to another. They might have issues initiating a process altogether. Remember that executive functioning, focus and attention are being built in the brain.[5] No one is born with perfectly functioning executive abilities like planning and organization.[6] Yet, imagine how a child's confidence can tumble when they think they should be able to finish a simple task or set of tasks without getting lost, but they can't. It is frustrating. With these students, the issue is compounded when they go to a progressive or non-traditional school. They are working in an unstructured environment, without modeling of basic study skills. They also lack the ability to follow through because their brain is still developing. How do they thrive and feel safe? It's maddening!

Issue #7: I have a teenager. Am I too late to make a difference?

We get calls from parents of 16-year-old teens struggling in high school completely panicked that their child is somehow done developing. They think the wiring is a foregone conclusion. According to Harvard University Neuroscientist Dr. Frances E. Jensen, the myth that your intelligence and IQ are fixed is just that—a myth.[7] Jensen argues that there is solid research to "show that your IQ can change during your teen years."[8] The brain is still forming. The prefrontal cortex, which controls awareness, planning, consequence, and urgency, is the last part of the brain to develop fully.[9]

It is now fairly common knowledge amongst educators, but most parents don't realize that brains don't fully form until about age 25. In neuroscience, they call the shaping of the brain from experience "plasticity."[10] It means that the brain is capable of change based on environment and experience. Pretty great news, right?

Now, What?

I hope we can help heal this "Culture of Perfectionism" and/or "overparenting" by doing the opposite—empowering you and other parents to let their kids be imperfect. We need to tighten the reins on technology, boundaries and routines. We need to loosen the reins on image, appearance and perfection. We need to let our kids try, fall down and even fail. We need to let them learn and we need to embrace them where they are at—imperfections and all. Parents need to stop over-parenting in certain areas and stop under-parenting in other areas so kids can fly solo and start to do for themselves. We need to teach children to see their mistakes not as catastrophic failures but as feedback: "it's okay that you are not good at calculus-not a big deal. Listen, I wasn't great at chemistry either but that didn't stop me from going to an Ivy League school." A mistake is an opportunity to strengthen a muscle. Sometimes that muscle is a math muscle, an SAT or ACT muscle or even a resilience muscle.

This book is the ideal guidebook for a parent that needs a hand to walk them step-by-step through the process of instilling strong habits, life skills and resilience. I use all my favorite meta-learning tools and blend them with a little tough love. Although, I assure you no one is slapping anyone's hand with a ruler. I give you all the science behind why each tool works so if you have a "child who loves to debate you at home" you have some ammo. Finally, I give you all my field experience.

Are you seeing major distraction? There is a tool for that. Are you noticing your child is avoiding their teacher? I can help. Is your child engaging in a lot of negative self-talk, check! Are you the parents having feelings about implementing structure? No problem. We will work through it.

HOW THIS WORKBOOK WORKS

The following chapters outline seven (7) critical habits and life skills that will help your student thrive in life.

You will notice that I talk a lot about school as well as study habits but school is their environment and their world. It is where our children learn the tools of the trade. They learn how to navigate their world. They learn the habits and skills that set the tone for the rest of their life.

The book is divided into three parts:

Part I is about creating the environment. The right environment is essential for a child to thrive. Chapter two is dedicated to creating the right environment so your child can be focused and organized with all the right tools at their fingertips.

Part II is about the right behaviors. Children don't know what they don't know. The four chapters in Part II help you create and model the right behaviors so that your child can feel confident and even get that A.

Part III is about the right mindset. With environment and behavior under control, we fine-tune attitude, positivity, and cooperation. Once we remove the stressors that create avoidance and evasiveness, we focus your child on how to get to the next level. Mindset is the key. We will work on activities that help your child think positively to create the best possible outcomes with all of their teachers, tutors, and other authority figures.

A SHOPPING LIST

Before we begin, get these items on the list below! They are the basics school supplies for children from the Third grade up:

1. 3 ring binder
2. Paper: lined
3. Paper: printer
4. Spiral bound notebooks
5. Pens: blue and black ink
6. Pencils: no. 2 (either mechanical or old fashioned)
7. Dividers

AUTHOR'S NOTE

This book is a roadmap for parents who need help closing the gaps in their child's development. It is a guidebook for those parents who need reassurance that their instincts are correct. You aren't crazy. Your children may not be getting the study skills and structure they need. I am in the trenches alongside you. I was scratching my head for a while wondering how to fix it until I figured out what was working with my clients.

This field guide gives you answers so that you can ask the right questions or close those gaps yourself.

1

BEFORE WE GET STARTED: CHARTING YOUR COURSE

"Begin with the end in mind"
-Stephen Covey

When a family starts with me, the first thing I always ask the parent is, "What is the goal?" The truth is I can tell a lot from how the parent answers this question. Some parents state very clearly, "We want an A." Some parents exclaim desperately, "We just need our child to pass." Others may share with me that the goal is purely "to build confidence."

Ultimately, what I (and my team) understand is that it is essential to set a short-term goal based on the immediate need. Typically a school will contact me when they have a student who has hit academic probation. Sometimes, there are multiple D's or multiple F's. The immediate short-term goal is to get the student to pass their class. Longer term, I set a goal to make the student thrive—to help nurture this child so that they can hit an even higher target.

I am such an optimist. I believe that every child given the right tools, the right practice, and the right coach can hit their highest potential. Of course, I always set my expectations realistically. I typically can get the child to pass within a few months of my coach entering the home. If money is no object, then I can even get the child to an A in the short term. But, the real magic happens in sustaining the A. My ultimate challenge is how can I turn this D or F student into a student who thrives permanently?

I always know that goal—thriving—takes time. Ninety percent of the time, I can get a client there in a few semesters. With more challenging cases, it takes longer. It depends on the student and the circumstances.

Those differences never stop me.

Making Up for Lost Time

Don't look backward. There is simply no point in crying over spilled milk. If your student is at an F, it's okay. If your child is struggling to enjoy reading, no problem. As the Buddhist monk Pema Chödrön always states, "Start where you are."[11] Her book by the same title is a guidebook to being compassionate with ourselves. The same is true for your children. This is a brilliant opportunity for a child to learn to become patient with themself. If you want to heal perfectionism, you need to embrace self-care and understanding. It's about learning to let go of what we think something should be in favor of what is. You will need to accept yourself and your kids as you are! Right here and right now. I will not judge you. No one is looking at you. One of the biggest things I had to learn as a recovering perfectionist, is that no one was judging me as harshly as I judged myself. You will find that the more you let go of what you think something should be and embrace what is working, the more you will actually thrive. You might even reach your goals more quickly with more ease.

Remind your child and remind yourself each day:

Life is a process. It's about progress towards the goal, not perfection.[12]

If you are familiar at all with 12-step recovery, this message of "progress not perfection" is often repeated in the rooms of any 12-step group. I am excited to be sharing wisdom I have picked up from many different sources throughout this book.

Say this as a mantra to yourself through this process. Say it each morning if you have to! We humans are bound to make mistakes. Each misstep is an opportunity to develop two very important life skills: self-compassion and self-forgiveness. You and your child only have the present! There is no sense in lamenting about the past.

LET'S GET STARTED: SET YOUR GOALS

This is a great time to sit down with your child and discuss goal setting. Remember to make goals as realistic and specific as possible.

Short-Term Goals

Your short-term goal is usually something attainable in a day or a week. Don't worry about whether it is necessarily something that is sustainable without continued support. We have to lay a foundation of good habits and good study skills to keep that confidence. We will focus on those longer goals below.

Example:

1.   Pass 8th grade algebra test
2.   Turn in homework on time
3.   Make my bed

What short-term goals have you and your child decided upon?

....

....

....

....

....

Long-Term Goals

Your long-term goals will be those goals that will take more sustained effort. These goals take continued fine-tuning over a longer period of time like a semester or a year.

Example:

1.   Encourage positive self-talk
2.   Participate in class
3.   Get an A in math

Write down a list of long-term goals for you and your child. What do you want to prioritize?

....

....

....

....

....

2

ENVIRONMENT IS EVERYTHING

"Happiness is when what you think, what you say and what you do are in harmony."
-Mahatma Ghandi

CASE STUDY A
Aaron, 4th grade

A local elementary school had contacted us with a referral: Aaron was a smart fourth grader who was underperforming on tests. His mom equally couldn't figure out what was wrong. She wanted to know what she could do to fix it. Upon entering the home, Aaron's mother very kindly ushered our tutor into her kitchen. She too was in the kitchen making dinner.

The tutor went along, making a notation in the written assessment. There was a cacophony of sounds: pots clanking, food packets ripping, and siblings yelling.

Even the tutor had trouble concentrating. When the tutor asked to move to a different room, the mom had said no. She wanted to observe what the tutor was doing. Presumably, she wanted to observe what my tutor was doing differently. Every time they would begin to complete a math problem, there was another loud noise to get them off track. Then, it was Aaron's younger brother. The student would begin working on yet another math problem and then—boom—he was interrupted by his younger brother with impunity.

Since this session was merely an assessment of Aaron and his environment, the tutor jotted down his concerns. Needless to say, the tutor called me the minute he left the home and shared that the environment was the biggest culprit.

Our fourth grader Aaron was working in a high

traffic kitchen filled with noises and interruptions. He was underperforming on his tests because he was distracted when he was trying to memorize!

CASE STUDY B
Bobbie, 5th grade

We had another young man Bobbie in 5th grade. As a two-household family, the family requested that we pick a neutral off-site environment where the student and the tutor could meet distraction-free. Bobbie's parents decided upon a local library. Although the library seemed like a good option—libraries in theory are quiet—the reality was that it wasn't free of distractions. One of the primary issues we had with Bobbie was that he was already inattentive.

The constant flurry of patrons in and out of the library was causing him to lift his head and stare instead of pay attention to his work. There were people on the computer click clacking away on the keys. Other patrons were talking. If Bobbie was going to find something to pull him away from his work, he had plenty of options. After observing the impact the environment had on the student, my tutor immediately suggested a new alternative.

We ended up moving to one of the parent's home and found a quiet office to work in. Ultimately, the move to a home office was the perfect solution. It was quiet, away from siblings and the high traffic areas of the house. Within a few months, this D student began flourishing to a B.

One of the cornerstones of my work in education has been about creating structure, order, routine and calm in children's lives so they have all the tools to thrive. I am sure it was pretty obvious that both Aaron and Bobbie in the case studies above had been struggling academically because of the distraction in their environments. Yet, these children are not alone. Where we do our work is as important as how we do our work. I have been shouting this from a soapbox for a long time, but there is actual science behind why we don't allow our kids to listen to music while they study. Or, why most of our parents frowned when we demanded to sit on the couch while we read a history textbook. It's not good for us!

State-Dependent Learning

State-dependent learning is the phenomenon that students learn and recall pieces of information better if they can approximate the same conditions in both the study (encoding) and testing (retrieval) environments.[13] We are more likely to remember something on a test if the conditions in the testing environment are similar to our study environment. Because testing environments are controlled by the school and are typically quiet and distraction free, we have to work backward to approximate this during study time. We as people have to be in the same emotional, physical, and mental state at the time of studying as the time of testing! It seems pretty straightforward. But, what does this mean for you as a parent? We are going to need to work backward!

A quiet study environment is best

In order to approximate testing conditions on test day, a calm study environment is the best. Other than the few students who might be rustling papers or tapping pencils, no one is blasting heavy metal music or singing out loud to the latest song when kids take tests—at least we hope not. Classrooms are quiet. There are other students, but those students are also quietly taking notes or taking a test. So, guess what that means for you as the parent? The room your child studies in must approximate that same level of quiet.

If your child has been working in high traffic areas like kitchens and living rooms, they are not conducive to your child doing well on their test. Beyond the distractibility of your child, students don't take tests in chaotic environments. If that is what has been happening until now, guess what— it definitely needs to change. Now, you might be thinking… but what if I have three kids? Well, they need to learn how to study quietly either together or separately in different areas of the house.

Or, you might be thinking: my house is a zoo. I have two

little ones that are always running around interrupting their older brother. Then, there are three options. Option 1: Set some ground rules about noise during homework time. Option 2: If you have little ones, take them outside to play during homework time. Option 3: Some combination of option 1 and option 2. This is a great time to teach all the members of the house respect for one another's needs.

It's hard to remember this but your kids are not in charge, you are! Often parents forget that kids don't need to like you all the time. You are there to help steer them in the right direction. As we move through these next few chapters, their desires often will be at odds with what is good for them. That's okay. They are kids. They don't know. That is why they have you—their parent.

SCIENCE TIME

The seminal study conducted by Godden and Baddeley in 1975 examined the relationship between memory and environment.[14] Several scuba divers were given a list of 36 words. Some memorized on land and some while in the water. If the scuba divers learned the words in water, they were more likely to recall the same list of 36 words while in water. If the scuba divers were on land while they encoded and memorized the words, they were more likely to remember the list while on land. However, the land group was less likely to recall those same words in water. Conversely, the scuba group who learned in water were less likely to remember the same list of words on land. Basically, if a person is tested in an environment that is dissimilar or incongruent to the place they learned or memorized the information, they are less likely to recall and remember what they learned.

Endnote 14

No background music and no TV!

Many parents call me telling me that their kids study while listening to music and/or watching television. This is a huge no-no! After reading above, you and I both know why! I warn them to get their kids away from those habits! Many teenagers make the argument that they can absolutely listen to music while doing homework or while studying. The argument I always hear: music relaxes them. Have you heard that argument from your teenager? Allow me to give you the real scientific evidence as to why music and TV are not helpful.[15]

SCIENCE TIME CONTINUED

Nick Perham and Joanne Vizard's 2010 study confirmed two points: First, studying can be enhanced by listening to music prior to studying to increase mood. Second, performance come test day is reduced if the person listens to music or distracting speech while performing the cognitive function.[16]

Perham and Vizard conducted an experiment in which the subjects were asked to memorize items under five conditions: quiet, music they liked, music they disliked, changing state speech (example: podcast or talk radio with changing volumes of speech) and non-changing state speech (monotone speech).

Despite liking the music, the participants performed equally low on recall tests whether they listened to music they liked or they hated. Changing speech—like talk radio—was also distracting! Having any sound variation during studying was enough to impact the quality of learning. The change in tones in the music or in speech was a distraction to the participant's ability to rehearse, memorize and eventually retrieve the data needed to be recalled. The participants actually learned best in quiet or monotone speech.

Endnote 16

Studying = No Headphones

Using this same reasoning, students, who test in quiet environments, need to memorize in quiet environments in order to yield the best results. Since it's rare that any teacher would allow students to wear headphones while taking a test, the chances are less likely that the student will perform to their best ability if they study with headphones on.

QUICK TIP: Do you have a child that likes a good debate? Does your child also question your authority or sources of information? This type of scientific research is just the right amount of ammunition to help an inquisitive child aka a "debator" get the information to answer their questions and calm their mind. It enables you to answer why it is perfectly fair for you to shut off their iPad or Spotify!

We learn better in the same space

Another benefit of establishing a routine homework environment is that we learn better in a routine location. We study better in the same location because of something called "place-dependent learning."[17] It's funny to even contemplate, but we have a better chance of remembering what we learned if we sit in the same place we learned it.[18] By the same token, we have a better chance of recalling something if we sit in a similar environment. This means our recall must be in similarly situated environments for optimal results.

So with that said...let's get to creating the right environment and the right routine.

LET'S GET STARTED: CREATE THE RIGHT ENVIRONMENT

When we begin with any family, we start with this essential goal:

Creating a "Study Space" where a coach from my company will do the work with your child every time they work together!

I usually have my team carve out a dedicated work-space in the home on the first appointment. I have them use a dining room or somewhere downstairs where the student can set up a basecamp of their materials. I don't permit coaching upstairs in a bedroom for legal reasons, but I also discourage studying in a bedroom because it can impact a student's sleep if the study and sleep are conducted in the same space.

So, the first thing we are going to do is designate a place in your home to set up a consistent Study Space!

WEEK 1: CREATING A ROUTINE WORK SPACE TO STUDY

We encourage parents to plant the seeds of routine gradually. Change can be tough! Remember this mantra as we move through these Study Space exercises:

I'm carving out space for my child's best learning!

A lot of these micro-steps should be done gradually over time in digestible bites so that we can remove resistance and master one step at a time.

ACTIVITY 1: Setting aside a "Study Space"

Much of the fun my staff and I have in our office is transmitting our love of learning to children. Since we meet with kids after school, sometimes my team is met with joy and sometimes frustration. Kids naturally want to stay away from a study environment. They also want to minimize any exposure to difficult areas. Rather than reinforce this mindset, I aim to get them to associate learning with fun and self-confidence! Part of getting children to re-set their anti-school mindset is to create a fun space where they can learn in the home.

I am not talking about a dreary old desk and a scary green lamp from your old college library. I mean to create an environment in which children will associate learning with you or with a third party.

Day 1: Picking the Study Space

I suggest a low traffic area of the house. Some families love their kitchen, but there are a lot of distractions in a kitchen. Remember Aaron from above! We suggest converting an under-used dining room or the old playroom into a child's study space. It's up to you and your family.

For older students, students between 7th and 12th grade, it's crucial that the study space is a room that is separate from the bedroom because it helps lessen anxiety and insomnia at bedtime when there are two separate areas for study and sleep.

Day 2: Setting Up a Study Space

I love a table and a big wall. I have had students set up the dining room, although that is not always popular with moms and dads. You will need a desk or a desk like surface. You will need shelves for textbooks and places to put away school supplies.

Day 3: Setting Up a Study Wall

What is a study wall? This is an area where the student will put up a large calendar of monthly events. But, between you and I, it is also the area where you will put up rewards, awards, and any areas of success. This is where you begin to showcase your child's growth so they can feel encouraged and supported on this journey.

Take time this week to break out each one of these activities: picking the study area, setting up the study area, and setting up the study wall.

Day 4 & 5: Study in Your Homework Zone

You are going to want to monitor progress on whether your child uses this area to actively study.

I am also going to suggest that you pick a Friday for picking the space and a Saturday for set up. Decorating and pulling together this space should be fun and engaging for you and your family!

Checklist

__ Day 1: Pick the study space

__ Day 2: Set up the study space

__ Day 3: Set up the study wall

__ Day 4: Utilize the study space

__ Day 5: Utilize the study space

QUICK TIP: In houses that are short on space, a rule about quiet time for homework will be especially important. But, all houses can benefit from creating homework boundaries for all siblings so that as each child finishes homework, they don't disturb their siblings.

PARENT REFLECTION

How did the first week of activities go?

....

....

....

....

Was your child resistant?

....

....

....

....

Did you implement it right away? How many days or weeks did you wait?

....

....

....

....

Were there any obstacles to picking or finding a quiet, distraction-free Study Space?

....

....

....

....

3

ROUTINE ISN'T THE ENEMY, CHAOS IS

"Creativity is a habit, and the best creativity is the result of good work habits."
-Twyla Tharp

CASE STUDY C
Caroline, 5th grade

Caroline had come to us from an elementary school. Her mother was beside herself. The teachers had told Caroline not to worry about memorizing her times tables. The information would come together over time.

Caroline's mother was not so sure. A great student in the first semester of 5th grade, Caroline was now consistently scoring Cs on her tests. Her confidence had taken a serious dip. On top of that, Caroline was fighting her mother on memorizing flashcards because the teacher had told her it wasn't necessary.

Caroline's mom was getting more and more concerned. She feared that as her daughter's 5th grade class moved further along in the second semester, she would be left behind. Caroline needed to know her basic times tables to excel at simplifying fractions or measurement.

We would experiment with introducing this traditional learning skill of memorization so that we might affect a change in Caroline's ability to do 5th grade math. Each week we routinely worked on this one task ever so slightly. Instead of telling the child her task was to "memorize" the tables, her tutor worked on games with the information on the cards. We wanted to remove "the negativity" and the pressure associated with "memorizing" the cards.

We never deviated from the task at hand. We stuck to

3: ROUTINE ISN'T THE ENEMY, CHAOS IS

times tables until she mastered them!

The results were astounding. Not only did Caroline do well, she began to get 100% on her tests. Her mother called us, ecstatic. It was a total turnaround.

Within 9 weeks of tutoring Caroline only one hour per week on her multiplication tables, she had scored an 18/22. She had gotten her first B- since 5th grade. This was a huge jump from earlier expectations. Not only was she less confused in class, but her confidence had jumped up dramatically. By week 10, she had received her first 100%. As a team, we were elated with her progress. Within 2 semesters, Caroline had become an entirely different student.

CASE STUDY D
Danielle, 11th grade

Danielle had been a new student of mine for only about a year when her mom had asked us to take over her ACT preparation. She booked a session on Sundays and a second session for math on Tuesdays. Danielle stayed consistent through her first month but her second and third months were filled with conflicts. As any sophomore or junior can attest, between sports, looming AP classes, SAT II's, club sports, and other commitments, conflicts crop up second semester. She took one test but did not perform as well as she hoped.

Her mother called to figure out: what wasn't working?

After some investigation, her mom and I realized that out of 16 sessions, 7 had been cancelled for matches and other conflicts. It was going to be a challenge to get into that routine! We decided as a team that Danielle would wait for her September ACT. She could begin more aggressive weekly preparation in her downtime—over the summer—in June, July and August.

Danielle made a deal with her tutor and her mom that she would then refocus in June, July and August. And...she did! She stuck to her planned sessions and her routine. When September came around, she went up to a 33 on her grammar section. She increased more than 7 points when she stuck to her routine!

Ah, structure! For some reason, we have come to associate words like "structure" and "routine" with the absence of freedom and creativity. Structure connotes images of totalitarian governments and old rigid teachers; 1950s videos of people in sad grey uniforms doing things like jumping jacks in unison. The images are authoritarian. It also evokes feelings of austerity. Words like "strict," "severe," "cold," "difficult," and "joyless." I could go on and on. But, I am a H-U-G-E cheerleader for structure. We want to help set up our children for success but often times we haven't implemented the right tools to help them down the road to getting there.

We need to *re*-consider how we think about structure and

routine. Structure is one of the most loving and compassionate things you can do for your child. It should actually evoke playing and jumping. It should elicit joy.

Routine and structure actually do the opposite of what some might think. They simulate feelings of safety. They foster trust. In a constantly changing world, they allow our children to feel safe. Why? Well, in a nutshell, creating structures and setting schedules allow our children to feel a modicum of predictability.

PREDICTABILITY = SAFETY

What is a Routine?

According to the Oxford Dictionary, a routine is a "set of actions regularly followed."[19] Like a dance routine, a morning routine could be a simple combination of behaviors such as getting up at 6:30 am, taking a shower, brushing one's teeth, drinking coffee, and having breakfast. These are activities done in an order repetitively.

Routines = Safety + Confidence

Here's the rub. Studies now show something that I have known for a while—regular routines increase levels of happiness and contentment.

I am going to say this again and again. I like sharing

resources. I read a great journal article—"Routine and Feelings of Safety, Confidence, and Well-Being."—in the *British Journal of Psychology* by Dinah Avni-Babad.[20] Her study supported everything I have seen with my boots on the ground—routines make us happy.[21]

Why? Classical Conditioning. This concept from psychology basically boils down to the idea that the more you do something, the easier it becomes. The easier something becomes, the more you like doing it. I thought this was mind-blowing in its simplicity.[22] According to Avni-Babad, "Cumulative evidence indicates that the mere exposure to stimuli leads to a change in affect towards those stimuli."[23] Avni-Babad states that as we increase our exposure to a certain person, place, or thing, we increasingly like it. Repeatedly doing something makes us warm up to it.

Example

Think about it this way. Imagine you take your child to an after-school activity each week; say a creative theatre class. It's the same group of children. It would be easy to estimate that certain children would enter the class guns blazing, extroverted, and ready to make friends. Other children might take a longer time to make friends. Typical stuff. You might also imagine that all of these kids will take time to warm up to each other. But the truth is that, over time, these children would feel an increased sense of safety towards each other and towards the teacher by virtue of the repeated exposure to each other.

A little backstory

It's funny, at the outset of my business, clients would call wanting help. Yet, they didn't understand the necessity of a weekly routine appointment at a set time. They would all ask, "Why? How would that work?" Their child had so many other obligations, they had dance every day at 4:00 p.m. followed by piano on some weeks but without a set schedule. Followed by family dinner....and, well, you get my drift. It would be next to impossible to find the time for the family to create a designated weekly study hour. Well, there you have it. There wasn't any time in the child's schedule to study. Is it any wonder that the child left little to no time for their studies? Of course not.

I have pretty much seen it all so I thought it might be helpful for you to identify where you—*the parent*—might be hitting roadblocks on the path to creating structure. The first thing we need to understand is your own "willingness." Are you willing to make your child's routines and good habits a priority in your life? A lot of our work starts and stops with basic "willingness" on the part of the family. We need to first eliminate your potential *unwillingness* to create routine.

LET'S GET STARTED: HOW WILLING ARE YOU TO CREATE STRUCTURE AND ROUTINE?

You might have already noticed there are several places where you will be documenting your experience as a parent on the road to getting your child on track. If you notice that you need more room to write, consider buying a journal. I have created a list below of questions to help you think through your roadblocks.

Let me tell you it took me a long time to make peace with routines. I thought I hated them but having a business where I needed to show up for young people counting on me made me change my ways!

For this short activity, please use the questions and statements below. Write all the fears and apprehensions you have about creating structure in your own life. What comes up?

Do you consider yourself to be "right brained" (creative/nonlinear)?

....

....

....

....

Do you consider yourself to be "scattered"?

....

....

....

....

Do you like to "go with the flow"?

....

....

....

....

Do you avoid setting routines in your own weekly schedule?

....

....

....

....

Do you feel overwhelmed or restricted by routine?

....

....

....

....

Do you agree with the statement "routine is anathema to creativity"?

....

....

....

....

Do you consider yourself to be a permissive parent?

....

....

....

....

Do you disagree with the statement "school is the number one priority in my child's life"?

....

....

....

....

Do you agree with the statement "sports/ drama/ art/ music/ etc. should play a major role in my child's life?"

....

....

....

....

If you answered mostly "yes," you may be more resistant to setting schedules and sticking to routines.

....

....

....

....

Do these results shock you?

....

....

....

....

Now, take a moment to journal about your fears surrounding setting routines.

PARENT TIME

We often focus so much of our attention on our tween or teen's resistance to routines. What about your own self-imposed barriers? It's a major trap not to consider your own relationship with routines and school in this process.

Let's examine some of our own roadblocks to success.

Roadblock #1: The Boundary Roadblock

Some parents resist setting routines. My staff will enter houses where there are no bedtimes, no study times and no dinner times. The parents worry their children will rebuff their attempts at routine. They don't want to create friction in the home. Some parents came from difficult and rigid homes. They had an authoritarian parent, a military parent, or a strict parent. They don't want to create the same environment for their own children.

Other parents express concerns that this type of structure doesn't work with their children. They tried it a few times, but it didn't stick. Their children are unable to even stick to the bedtime.

Does this sound like you or your family?

Roadblock #2: The Memory/Mental Roadblock

In the early days, parents came to me who had set up mental roadblocks against their children studying. In fact, one of the problems I identified in the early days was the "family-thinking" towards studying in general. What dawned on me is that so many parents had their own relationship with school... and it wasn't necessarily positive. Many moms or dads had their own difficulty with academics. They struggled with the social component. Alternatively, they disliked the rigidity of the school environment. They had created their own negative associations with the "rigidity" of school. So, what do they do? These parents respond to their own negative experience by striving to give their children the opposite—non-routine—experience.

With the best intentions, these parents, who were potentially unsuccessful in a school environment, strip away everything that they identified as harmful in their own experience. They do the opposite and promote no schedule. They might also promote non-academic achievements so they can insulate their children from whatever negativity they had experienced. In some families, this manifests as over-scheduling of other non-academic engagements. Whether it is dance, theatre, sports, or a combination of all three, sometimes parents de-prioritize school in an attempt to protect their kids. They aren't that interested in their children being academic. It's not the priority. Does this sound like you?

Roadblock #3: The Commitment Roadblock

Many of our families, however, just don't understand how their child received a D or F. They just don't understand how it happened under their watch. They are equally confused by my company's policies. Why isn't my company like all the other tutoring companies? Why can't my clients book one appointment at a time? They want to be able to come and go as they please.

They want to come in right before a test because they heard that my method helps with recall and retention. Perhaps even the night before the test and cross their fingers hoping their child can cram the information in and get a better grade. Many of these parents also want to work with us weekly but don't want to commit to a weekly routine session at a set time. They don't operate that way. It is difficult for them to commit.

Sometimes parents refuse to get on board. They walk away angry. How could I turn away a paying client? Shouldn't they be able to just book us when and where they wanted to? In these cases, the parents also suffer from some level of disorganization themselves. Either mom or dad has trouble sticking to schedules and routines, so it trickles down to the child or children.

Does this sound like you?

This is a judgment-free zone so if you have identified something you relate to, that's great! We all have hurdles and roadblocks that need to be addressed head on.

WHY ARE ROUTINES IMPORTANT?
Routines Save Energy & Increase Relaxation

The additional benefit of creating a routine is that the repetition of a behavior feels relaxing. Once a child has created a study area and a set time to study, there is no thinking involved in where they will study or at what time. Children will begin to associate the time and the space with their work. According to Avni-Babad: "The automaticity of routine feels relaxing and saves energy. It is like switching from the active gear to the inactive one while still moving. [With] routines, there are no energy-consuming decisions to be made and no thoughts to invest." [24]

Routine Activities Foster Increased Positivity

When any child does something over and over again each week, it gets easier. The increased exposure to a certain stimulus increases improvement. Your child feels confident that they can do it! But, people often stop doing something they enjoy after experiencing something negative while doing it. Avni-Babad states that:

"In line with the theorizing about the mere exposure phenomenon, when people develop a routine behaviour, the routine choice would not continue if they would experience a negative event, but the lack of aversive consequence would perpetuate the routine practice and its concomitant positive affect." [25]

Conversely, the absence of a negative experience most certainly means the routine will continue!

This tendency to drop something that feels bad is what we want to work through. If you are wondering when we get to that skill, I want to assure you that we will address resilience building in Chapter 7 in a few weeks.

For now, what you need to know is that reducing your child's negative experiences will make it more likely that they are going to stick to the routine! That is why you, or a third party, are helping them work through these skills. By providing support with a troublesome task like practicing piano regularly or doing homework on time, you can remove or reduce the negativity. In turn, by reducing negative experiences, you increase the likelihood your child will continue with the routine!

But...what would happen if we entirely *remove* negative associations?

Routines Also Foster Enjoyment

We now know that routines become easier over time,

but what happens when we remove negative associations with the routine? In the absence of negative associations, the routine becomes enjoyable! Accountability partners and instructors don't solely help facilitate the routine, they remove the negative stressors so that you enjoy your routines. Psychologist and researcher Robert B. Zajonc proposes that routinely doing something makes you like it.[26] But it is the absence of any negative consequence or effect that makes the entire experience positive.[27] This is known as unconditioned stimulus.[28] In a nutshell, when you do something repetitively, you like it, but it is the absence of any negative experience that makes you really *enjoy* it, consider it a positive experience and continue doing it.

Example

Let's put this into practice: your child is characteristically shy. They prefer never to raise their hand. They do not often participate in class willingly. It is only when they are truly confused do they ever raise their hand. Their math teacher often has difficulty explaining the problem in a way that makes sense to your child. Your child then begins to associate raising their hand with confusion. They also pair the feeling of raising their hand with shame and fear. As you can imagine, they are not likely to participate in math or any class because the association between raising their hand and being confused has become classically conditioned with shame. The only way out of this loop is for your child to raise their hand when they are certain of the answer or have something interesting to add. While we can't "undo" the prior learning, we can introduce a new positive association using the same classical conditioning that caused the problem in the first place.

Example 2

Let's use calculus as a second example of a subject that has become associated with negativity. The tutor goes to the client's home every week at 5:00 p.m. to study calculus. The repeated exposure to calculus immediately reduces the severe anxiety associated with the subject. As the weeks progress, the tutor notices that the student makes similar errors in many problems and helps the student notice and correct the mistakes. As the student begins to recognize that her mistakes are fixable and that she can catch these mistakes on her own, she builds confidence and positivity. In the absence of new negative associations, the student will begin to actually LIKE calculus. I know this may sound like a stretch, but it actually happens!

Routines Create a Sense of Safety

The first thing I do at the outset of a client relationship is set a weekly appointment. Why? Our goal is to create that sense of weekly routine. Because when something becomes routine, it becomes easier to do and more likely to happen. My work with my clients is not about the short-term gain. It's about modeling positive behavior.

When my coach shows up every week at a client's house at 5:00 p.m. on Monday, it creates a safe trusting relationship between the student and the coach. The student knows they can rely on this mentor to show up every week at that time. The regularity and the consistency breed confidence in the coach. At a cellular level, it tells the student, I can count on this time and on this person.

Routine is Essential for the Learning Process

Routines are an essential part of my Ladder Method. I base so many of my skills on the basic idea that if I can lay out a routine for a child of multiple healthy habits, that child will thrive. Because thriving and cultivating what I call a Success Mindset is just implementing a set of healthy habits daily.

In addition to creating a sense of success, routine behaviors encourage new neural pathways and increase blood flow to the brain. According to Dr. Jensen from above, young minds are not merely the product of genetics, they are strongly shaped by experience.[29] In other words, young minds are shaped by the way they are nurtured. Jensen states, "The more a piece of information is repeated and relearned, the stronger the neurons become...."[30] So aside from creating positivity and fostering enjoyment, routine truly facilitates the learning process.

Many parents come to us upset that they told their child to do something once, twice or even three times. Often, parents blame the child or themselves for what they perceive is some inadequacy in their child. They forget that children are still developing. They are not adults. They are children who need to be reminded gently *and* often. They need the routine reinforcement. They aren't being bad intentionally. They are kids!

When I began working with kids, I remember sometimes forgetting and even getting impatient. Until I heard someone speak on a different topic: addiction. Something clicked that day. I changed my baseline. Instead of wondering why some of my worst cases weren't getting it right away, I looked at the overall month or few weeks. I started to look at things differently. I would ask myself: *Have there been more good days and productive days than unproductive days?* Or, if a bad behavior reared its ugly head, I would acknowledge it almost as if the child had fallen off the proverbial wagon. A bad habit takes time to unlearn! It's like a crutch.

I changed my entire measuring stick. It was not about punishing the child for falling off the proverbial wagon. It was about helping the child get back on. Change doesn't click for everyone in the same way or on the same timeline.

When you get frustrated, I want you to say this to yourself:

Routines aren't built in one day, It's about having more good days than bad days.

To learn new information, children need both frequency and recency.[31] They cannot study the night before the exam. They can't change a bad behavior overnight. They need to see the information or do something over and over. They need to do things often and over a longer period of time. They need things routinely repeated over and over again. Catch my drift? The more that children do their homework at a set time, the more likely they will be to do homework at all. But, they need constant, even daily, reinforcement.

Wait, Schedules do not Discourage Creativity?

Many parents come to me concerned that setting a strict routine or creating a weekly schedule will diminish their child's creativity. If Avni-Babad was not enough to convince you of the value of routine, let me share something I read in Mason Currey's book about artists and their routines: *Daily Rituals: How Artists Work.*[32] If you haven't read his book, go buy it. It's short. You can pick it up and put it down. I want to share with you Mason Currey's anecdotes and findings. It assuaged my lingering concerns.

All creative types work on a routine! Yes, it was all there in black and white. Creative artists, painters, authors and scientists all follow a set schedule each day and each week. All of the creatives mentioned in the book were creatures of habit, even if the habits looked a little different.

Picasso? Would it surprise you to learn that he painted every day and at the same time—2:00 p.m.[33] He painted every day without fail. He also only socialized on a specific day—Sunday.[34]

Would it surprise you to learn that Ernest Hemingway had a routine? He is so often thought of as a "messy" author and a heavy drinker. According to his reports, he always got up at 5:30 or 6:00 a.m and spent his morning writing, whether he drank heavily the night before or not.[35] When he was unable to write, or had a tough writing day, he would do other things like return correspondences. [36]

Famously creative and disheveled scientist Albert Einstein also had a daily routine. He would eat his breakfast in the late morning at roughly 9:00 a.m. and then head to work at Princeton promptly by 10:30 a.m. By the early afternoon, he would head home to nap. He took naps during the middle of day, but he did it routinely. [37]

Dancer Twyla Tharp was obsessive about her routine. Tharp even penned a book called *The Creative Habit* detailing her theory that consistency is essential to her dancing and creating.[38] Her theory is that "repetition" of her routines was the cornerstone of her life and certainly her life as a dancer.

Renowned poet and author Maya Angelou also had a daily routine that always started early at 6:00 a.m. in the morning with coffee.[39] After that she wrote outside of her home by 7:00 a.m. sharp. She would finish no later than 2:00 p.m.[40] She would edit her work in the afternoon until her husband came home for dinner. She then enjoyed the rest of her evening with him.

Funny enough, most, if not all, of these creative types were not very social, keeping mostly to themselves. Their personal lives looked slightly even anti-social. Instead, their lives were dedicated entirely to their creativity and the routines they had built around their passions whether they were artists or scientists.

A HYPOTHETICAL:

Imagine there are two children in the same lower-level reading group in a third-grade class. Because this is the lower reading group, the parents receive an email at the beginning of the school year requesting that the parents incorporate nightly reading into their routine.

Scenario 1:

Parent A elects to have his son read whenever he feels like it. Since Parent A is not often home and has engagements out for work most nights, his son has the ultimate freedom to decide when he can read. Parent A might read one night at 6:00 p.m. before dinner. The next night he might read with his son just before bed. Each night, the child has no idea whether he will have his father's help with the reading. He may read at 6:00 p.m. He may read at 8:00 p.m. Or not at all. In this scenario, the child's focus is on whether or not he will receive help, rather than on what he is actually reading. The child's focus is pulled into a different direction for lack of routine. When the parent shows up to parent-teacher conferences, he is informed that his child will not be moving up to the next reading level. Parent A is shocked and goes so far as to wonder whether his child has some kind of reading disability. He remains puzzled as to why his child remains in the lower reading group. Meanwhile, Student A reports that he hates reading and that he knows he will never be a "good" reader.

Scenario 2:

Imagine now that Parent B with an equally busy schedule gives his daughter a set reading schedule. He will read with her Mondays, Wednesdays, and Sundays at 8:00 p.m. He also schedules reading at the same time on Tuesdays and Thursdays to be completed on her own. Although he is not home every night, she knows which nights are their reading nights and which nights she reads on her own. She has a sense of safety that she knows when she can expect him to show up and when she should not expect him. She has a sense of the quantity or set numbers of time required for her reading. She also knows when to expect that they will read. Child B is then able to create a set routine and set other activities around this existing schedule. This child is also able to direct all her focus and energy toward the reading. At student B's parent-teacher conferences, the results are different. Because Parent B has stuck to the routine, he is already well aware that his daughter has improved in her reading comprehension over the past few months. Child B is moved to the mid-level reading group and Parent B continues to work with her using the same schedule. Student B reports looking forward to reading with her dad and is always eager to show him how much she can read on her own on their off days.

Good habits and routines are like anything else. It's a building block system. There are so many individual layers that need to be processed. Asking your child to go to bed at 8:30 p.m. one night and then expecting to them to do that each night routinely without prompting is like asking them to play a concerto after only practicing their scales for a few weeks. It would be entirely unfair.

Becoming a child who thrives requires dedication. It requires a weekly commitment of several hours. Most children involved in club teams practice up to 10 hours a week and play a game or two over the weekend. Yet, many of those parents don't seem to make the connection that a Success Mindset takes equal parts dedication.

The second thing I do is to set the routine day and time

for meeting with someone from my staff. It's time to get started creating that success-building routine!

LET'S GET STARTED: BUILDING A ROUTINE

WEEK 2: DESIGNATING A SET STUDY TIME

In Week 1, we encouraged you as parents to make sure that your child used your Study Space diligently. In the second week, you will set a specific study time into your weekly schedule. Remember, change is not always easy, especially for children. If they have been doing things "on their own schedule," adjusting to a fixed schedule may be a welcomed relief, or you might be met with mixed feelings: relief, apprehension, resistance or fear. You may be met with all four feelings simultaneously! It is about patience. Remember your mantra from above:

Routines aren't built in one day!
It's about having more good days than bad days.

Study time, ironically, may take some time to implement. We suggest reasoning with your child and explaining that the sooner their homework gets done, the sooner they can eat dinner. Play with their siblings. Play with a new toy. Watch their favorite program. Talk with their friends.

What we are trying to do is set certain behavior patterns upfront so that children routinely complete all their work when they get home. Over time, they will see that taking this approach and getting homework done early on will actually free up their mental and emotional energy for better work-life balance!

ACTIVITY 2:
Get out Your Calendar and Pick Homework Times

Kids and teenagers have a multitude of competing priorities. Between soccer, club, guitar, et al, it can be hard to figure out what the best time might be. We suggest that you give your child a short break after they get home from school or after school activities for a snack—between 15 and 20 minutes. Then, they should do homework right away. It is ideal if they could do it at roughly the same time each night as well.

Why? It can be difficult to get kids to settle back down if they get home and begin playing with their siblings.

Day 1: If it's 3:45 p.m. that they arrive home, give them until about 4:00 p.m. or 4:15 p.m. to eat a quick snack. If they have after school activities that may push your time back to 5:15 p.m. Make sure you stick to that homework time each day of the week. Remember, the more that your child hits the books at a single time, the more likely he or she will automatically get that work done at that time.

Day 2: Repeat homework time.

Day 3: Repeat homework time.

We ask that you work on the set homework time for two weeks. I know, it's crazy amount of time. But, we want to focus on the basics and fundamentals before we load your son or daughter up with too many changes in their current day.

Day 4: Repeat homework time

Day 5: Repeat homework time

	MON	TUE	WED	THU	FRI
3:00 p.m.					
3:30 p.m.					
4:00 p.m.					
4:30 p.m.					
5:00 p.m.					
5:30 p.m.					
6:00 p.m.					
6:30 p.m.					
7:00 p.m.					

WEEK 3: CREATING A WEEKLY ROUTINE OR SCHEDULE

ACTIVITY 3:
Create a Weekly Calendar

The next activity we always do with a new tutoring student, whether they are in 5th grade or in 10th grade, is help them create a weekly calendar or routine of multiple priorities like homework, dinnertime and bedtime.

We suggest taking calendars by the week. There is a great empty calendar that is available on iMac. You could also use Google calendars or a good-old fashioned planner.

Take the planner and begin putting in school times, then homework times, then sports practice, other activities, and then dinnertime and bedtime. Now that you have laid out what times they should eat and go to bed, you need to enforce those dinnertimes and bedtimes.

I realize that a lot of parents tend to have guilt about enforcing these rules because they don't have all the facts but now that you are armed with information, it should feel much less challenging.

High School Example

	MON	TUE	WED	THU	FRI
7:00-8:00	Breakfast	Breakfast	Breakfast	Breakfast	Breakfast
8:00-9:00	English	Geometry	English	Biology	English
9:00-10:00					
10:00-11:00	Free	History	Geometry	History	Geometry
11:00-12:00	Advisory				
12:00-1:00	Lunch	Lunch	Lunch	Lunch	Lunch
1:00-2:00	Biology	Art	Biology	Free	Art
2:00-3:00				School Meeting	
3:00-4:00	Break/ Snack	Break/ Snack	Break/ Snack	Break/ Snack	Break/ Snack
4:00-5:00	Home-work time	Piano lesson	Home-work time	Piano lesson	Home-work time
5:00-6:00		Piano lesson		Home-work time	
6:00-7:00					
7:00-8:00	Dinner	Dinner	Dinner	Dinner	Dinner
8:00-9:00	Practice piano	Study time	Practice piano	Study time	Practice piano
9:00-10:00	Wind-Down/ Bedtime	Wind Down/ Bedtime	Wind Down/ Bedtime	Wind Down/ Bedtime	Wind Down/ Bedtime

Now try creating your own...

	MON	TUE	WED	THU	FRI
7:00-8:00					
8:00-9:00					
9:00-10:00					
10:00-11:00					
11:00-12:00					
12:00-1:00					
1:00-2:00					
2:00-3:00					
3:00-4:00					
4:00-5:00					
5:00-6:00					
6:00-7:00					
7:00-8:00					
8:00-9:00					
9:00-10:00					

WEEK 4: BUILDING THE "ROUTINE" MUSCLE

ACTIVITY 4:

This week's activity is about making sure your son or daughter is doing work in the Study Space. We are also making certain that they are sticking to their scheduled homework, dinner and bed times.

	MON	TUE	WED	THU	FRI
Did your child study during the scheduled time today?					
Did she/he study at the designated location?					
If the answer to either question is no, what got in the way?					
How well did they stick to the calendar overall?					
How is having structure affecting you and your child?					

PARENT REFLECTION: CREATING A ROUTINE TIME TO STUDY, TO EAT AND TO SLEEP

How did this week's activity go for you?

....

....

....

....

Was your child resistant?

....

....

....

....

Did you implement this right away? If not, why not?

....

....

....

....

How were you at maintaining the study space?

....

....

....

....

WEEK 5: NO CHANGES IN ANY ROUTINE

ACTIVITY 5:
Continue working on routines, reinforcing the good behavior.

You are strictly going to monitor your child's habits and help them stick to the routine times. Here we are going to do more self-evaluation. You will make no changes in their current routine.

	MON	TUE	WED	THU	FRI
Did your child study during the scheduled time today?					
Did she/he study at the designated location?					
If the answer to either question is no, what got in the way?					
How well did they stick to the calendar overall?					
How is having structure affecting you and your child?					

PARENT/CHILD JOINT REFLECTION: CREATING A ROUTINE TIME TO STUDY, TO EAT & TO SLEEP

Have you and your child write down what you are most proud of for these last five weeks, as well as something you are most grateful for.

What did I do well!	What I am grateful for
What things I noticed	

PARENT REFLECTION: CREATING A ROUTINE FOR YOUR CHILDREN

How did these last five weeks of routines go?

....

....

....

....

Was your child resistant at any point?

....

....

....

....

Did you keep up the habits continuously?

....

....

....

....

Did you do anything differently than what was prescribed by the workbook?

....

....

....

....

If yes, what got in your way of creating a solid routine?

....

....

....

....

How were you at maintaining the study space?

....

....

....

....

4

FOCUS, FOCUS, FOCUS: GET RID OF DISTRACTIONS

"Focus is about saying no"
-Steve Jobs

CASE STUDY E
Ellie, 9th grade

Ellie came to our company this past school year. She was getting Ds in both biology and algebra. But, it was early in the school year, so I wasn't quite alarmed. I knew we had time to affect a change. Ellie had created her "study area" in part of her house, well away from the prying eyes of her mother and father. Against the coach's request, she kept her phone out and kept her notifications on. The issue hit a zenith when her parents were out of town. Ellie broke every one of my technology rules. She kept her phone out. She kept her notifications on. At the break, she even got on the phone. As you might guess, she never mentally returned to the session. You might be wondering just how much homework were they able to achieve in an hour and a half? Answer: Less than half of the math assignment they were supposed to complete.

After getting her parents involved upon their arrival back in LA, the phone was taken away. Now, guess how much homework and studying was achieved in the hour and a half? An entire math assignment and all of her biology reading! They tripled the amount of homework they were able to get done. Not surprising!

We arrive at the single most pressing issue facing parents in the Perfection Age—focus *and* technology. Many parents come to me entirely perplexed about how to implement screen rules. Many of these same parents lament about how to enforce screen rules when their children are forced to use technology for school homework and projects.

Your child may insist that they can multi-task. They may argue we now belong to a new culture of "multi-taskers." I am sure you have read one of the many articles out there. There is a gigantic list of them. There are also those rare educators who claim that we have evolved! These researchers posit that this next generation—Generation Z—is a technology generation.[41] The newest generation can, according to these theorists, play music, talk on the phone, and focus all at the same time. But, is that true?

Even Facebook's most notable founders and employees worry about the effects of social media and technology on children's brains.[42] As recently as May of 2019, Sean Parker, the former president of Facebook and one of its most notable investors, spoke out against social media stating: "God only knows what it's doing to our children's brains."[43] Facebook's former head of growth equally condemned that social media was: "ripping apart the social fabric of how society works."[44] Not great support for the idea that our children's brains are successfully adapting to technology, texting and social media! If you remember the study by Nick Perham from above, merely having music on is enough to affect a child's performance on test day.[45] Imagine what a flurry of social texts might do to your child in the middle of completing homework!

I think it's also pretty relevant to learn that tech giants like Bill Gates and Steve Jobs raised their children in technology-free environments. According to an article in *The Independent*, Bill Gates imposed a cap on screen time when his daughter developed an addiction to video games.[46]

Both Gates and Jobs raised their children with limited access to the technology they brought into your home. If you haven't read Nick Bilton's *New York Times* article "Steve Jobs Was a Low-Tech Parent" you need to![47] Bilton uncovered the fact that many, if not most, tech leaders limit the amount of technology consumed by their children.[48]

Bilton saw a gigantic disparity between tech and non-tech parents. Non-tech parents were far more likely to give their kids phones as early an age as 8.[49] *Eight!* Tech leaders were more likely to wait until the child was in their teens, as late as 14.[50] Bilton stated: "While these teenagers can make calls and text, they are not given a data plan until 16. But there is one rule that is universal among the tech parents I polled: There are no screens in the bedroom period. Ever."[51] Evan Williams, the founder of Blogger, Twitter, and Medium, according to Bilton, buys his children paperback books in lieu of books on Kindle or iPad.[52] Tech leaders like Gates and Jobs were well aware of the addictive natures of these devices. It's time to start following their lead.

Of course, you might think to yourself: "modern technology is not a Perfection Age problem." Before iPhones, there was TV. Before TV there was radio. It's not that there haven't existed distractions. I believe that what everyone needs to remember is that never have there been this *many* distractions, or this style of distraction.

It's not rocket science. All of those notifications from your child's friends on their computer, tablet, phone, or even watch interrupt your child's train of thought. One of the biggest ideas for this book was the almost constant discussion amongst my families about phones and notifications. I often chuckle to myself when a young teen tells me they can study and play music with lyrics at the same time. My golden rule is that when one of my coaches arrives at your door, the phone, the music, and the computer notifications must be turned off. But, imagine how distracting it is when the coach leaves.

PARENT TIME

This is a great time to also reflect on your own relationship to your phone, computer or social media. It's easy to get frustrated with your children but I often say that if you want your child to adopt the right habits, it starts with modeling the right behavior. Do you find *yourself* with the TV on, the computer out and the notifications on your phone on?

Take this time to answer the following set of questions. Remember this is not about self-judgment. It's a gut check to understand how all of the members of your family engage with technology!

Fill in the following chart about your own technology usage.

	Rarely	Daily	3+ times per day	For work only	More than I want to admit
Cell Phone					
iPad					
Television					
Computer					
Instagram					
Facebook					
Other					

Now answer the following questions:

Do you allow devices at the dinner table?

....

....

....

....

How often do your children observe you on social media?

....

....

....

....

What about the phone?

....

....

....

....

How do you use FaceTime? Do you engage with family?

....

....

....

....

Are you obligated professionally to be on your phone 24/7? Or on call?

....

....

....

....

Do any of your answers surprise you?

Multi-tasking slows down time spent on tasks & homework

Many parents have called me complaining that homework is taking their child well over 5 hours or that their child is barely able to study. They will lament and ask me, "What do you think might be causing all of this delay? Is my child being assigned too much homework?" Are the teachers too hard at my kid's school?

SCIENCE TIME

In a 2008 unpublished dissertation, LingBei Xu measured the reading comprehension of multiple graduate students when they were interrupted by IMing. Would you be surprised to learn that these graduate students didn't necessary have difficulty comprehending what they were reading? Rather, it took them 1.5 to 1.77 times longer to finish each reading![53] They understood what they were reading but they had to spend significantly longer to get that understanding. Imagine that if it takes a graduate student, without IM on, one hour to complete a reading, it takes that same student nearly 2 hours to complete the same task with IM on.

Endnote [53]

My answer to my parents' questions is always the same: it's not the homework! Your child is too distracted to get their work done efficiently. The tasks they complete are either littered with mistakes or are being done more slowly because your child is getting pinged on IM, on Instagram, and on their phones as they sit and read. Pretty distracting, right?

No wonder it's taking your child 5 hours to complete a set of assignments that should only take them 2 hours!

Multi-tasking does not exist

The most common myth I, and noted scientists, have to bust is the idea that children can successfully multitask.[54] Let me say it clearly: multi-tasking does *not* exist. Professors Paul A. Kirschner and Aryn Karpinski studied the effects of Facebook on performance.[55] The results are not positive! When we humans think we are multi-tasking, we are not.[56] According to Kirschner and Karpinski, you or your child are instead "switching quickly from one activity to another."[57] Humans are not able to multitask complex processes simultaneously. They can only do things simultaneously that are "automated." For example, humans and young teens can walk and chew gum. But humans cannot drive and talk on the phone successfully at the same time.

I found it equally important to share that Kirschner and Karpinski don't simply reference their own study, they also reference street tests from Car and Driver that I am going to share here. According to the National Highway Transportation Safety Administration, at least 300,000 accidents are caused by "distracted drivers."[58] In the Car and Driver article cited in Kirschner's work, the results of a street test involving humans showed that texting was as dangerous if not more dangerous than driving while intoxicated.[59] Did you know that distracted drivers—drivers using a cell phone to talk, read a text, or send a text—cause one out of four accidents?[60] I didn't! Given that it is impossible to drive while texting, imagine how much texting distracts your child from any task at hand. Learning requires more concentration than driving!

The next response I get is, "Well, then tell this to my kid who thinks they can multitask!" Here are the biggest ways to incentivize your children. Tell them: (1) it's going to take them three times as long to do the work (and the product isn't going to be half as good), (2) it means they have to stay up later to do work, (3) they wind up with less time talking to their friends and (4) it means the coach has to stay longer. No teen or tween wants their coach to stay any longer than they need to. Trust me!

Multi-tasking = More Mistakes

Multi-tasking doesn't only slow us down, it also leads to more mistakes. A student's performance also dips when students have to multi-task. Remember Xu's dissertation study in the paragraph above? Xu asked his group of students to collaborate in teams on a project where they would have to communicate through IM and Skype.[61] The person who was placed in the position of having to multitask items usually rated their performance as "satisfactory."[62] However, in the same circumstances, their teammates often gave that partner much lower marks than they gave themselves.[63] In other words, they are not able to properly gauge their own effectiveness.

So now what?

Now that you are armed with more information, you might not feel *so* guilty implementing screen rules. You aren't being unfair. You're being healthy! Your mantra needs to be:

I am helping my child develop healthier habits around technology because I now know better.

One of the biggest hurdles I face as the owner of a Meta-learning company is removing the distractions, so for our next set of exercises, we are going to implement screen rules! That's right. We are going to begin to create healthy relationships to technology.

LET'S GET STARTED: CREATING HEALTHY HABITS AROUND TECHNOLOGY

WEEK 6:

This week we are going to observe your child's relationship to technology. This is where the rubber hits the road and we get to discover what your child's habits really are!

Remember, we aren't trying to change anything right now. We are creating a baseline. I encourage parents to plant the seeds of good behavior gradually. We are going to work up to progress. Remember that change takes time.

QUICK TIP: One of the things we do at our company is model ideal cellular phone use in the session, putting our screens away when we work with a child so that the child can see and experience our full focus.

ACTIVITY 6: No changes in any Technology Habits

You are strictly going to monitor your child's technology habits and the time it takes them to complete tasks. Here we are going to do more evaluation. You are going to ask your child how long it takes to complete certain tasks. For younger students, this will be easy because you can oversee homework but for your older children, it will take some communication. You are going to ask them to write down for a whole week how long it takes to do each assignment. You will make no changes in their current habits.

	MON	TUE	WED	THU	FRI
How long did your child predict homework and studying would take today?					
How long did your child actually spend doing homework and studying today?					
If there was a major discrepancy, what factors do you think led to the difference?					
Is your child using the designated study space and study time?					

PARENT REFLECTION: DISTRACTIONS & OBSERVATIONS

Now, take a moment to journal about your experience so far. Since this is an observation week, it's important to assess. Remember, your mantra:

I am helping my child develop healthier habits around technology because I now know better.

You might be alarmed at what you see given what you have read. You may also want to make changes guns blazing. I am going to ask you not to. Right now, you are going to observe your child. This is also a great opportunity to take stock of what you have been doing that is working!

How did this observation week go?

....

....

....

....

Did you think about your own relationship to technology?

....

....

....

....

What kind of rules were you inspired to create?

....

....

....

....

Do you already have any existing blocks or parental controls on internet, social media or television?

....

....

....

....

Do you have any pre-existing rules about what age your child can get a phone?

....

....

....

....

What about a data plan?

....

....

....

....

What about a rule on what age your child can have an Instagram account?

....

....

....

....

If you answered no to many of the questions above, did you feel you wanted to immediately jump in to create screen rules with your child?

....

....

....

....

What is going well thus far?

....

....

....

....

What are some improvements you are seeing?

....

....

....

....

What did you notice that is being done differently? Done well?

....

....

....

....

What was challenging?

....

....

....

....

WEEK 7: SCREENTIME & HOMEWORK

ACTIVITY 7: Screen Rule 1.0
No phones, notifications or chat for 1 hour of study time.

I know that children may freak, but the no phone, no notifications and no chat rule is completely paramount to helping your child develop healthy technology habits.

Ask your child to study with no break, no phone, no tablets, and no electronics for 1 hour. Technology may be a reward after they hit the one hour mark. We start with 1 hour because that is the minimum time that a coach would expect to work with an elementary student.

What you are going to do is communicate with your children. You are going to ask how long it took them to complete assignments in the given time slot. Again, with smaller children this is about getting them to learn to put down electronics to build those good habits! You will be able to see how long it takes them to complete standardized tasks.

With older children, this is about self-reflection. Challenge your student to try to do the work without those distractions!

	MON	TUE	WED	THU	FRI
Was your child able to work for the whole hour without distractions?					
If no, what was the source of the distraction?					
How long did your child predict homework and studying would take today?					
How long did your child actually spend doing homework and studying today?					
Is your child using the designated study space and study time?					

PARENT REFLECTION: SCREEN RULE 1.0

Now, an hour can seem so short but for children who have been weaned on *Siri™* and *Alexa™*, a few minutes can feel like a lifetime.

How did this week go?

....

....

....

....

Did you try the screen rule yourself?

....

....

....

....

What is going well? What was a positive outcome?

....

....

....

....

What was challenging?

....

....

....

....

Did they get emotional without their technology?

....

....

....

....

QUICK TIP: If you feel like your child is struggling with screen rules and you don't want to become the "technology police," you may want to consider bringing in a neutral accountability partner, coach or tutor who can help establish this routine for you.

WEEK 8: SCREENTIME & HOMEWORK

ACTIVITY 8: Screen Rule Version 2.0
No phones for 1.5 hours of homework time.

We are gradually increasing the time spent away from their devices so we can see how hard or how easy it is to pry them away from technology. How deep is the dependency?!

The added bonus is that we also reduce the time that your child could get hit with pieces of information to "react" to.

We had a student where we had to monitor her usage because she was so sensitive that the slightest bad news or social issue could derail her productivity and her mood!

	MON	TUE	WED	THU	FRI
Was your child able to work for the whole hour and a half without distractions?					
If no, what was the source of the distraction?					
How long did your child predict homework and studying would take today?					
How long did your child actually spend doing homework and studying today?					
Is your child using the designated study space and study time?					

QUICK TIP: Depending on how "addicted" to screens your child may be, you may want to extend the hour and a half for a few more weeks before moving forward to extending the "no screens" time.

PARENT REFLECTION: SCREEN RULE 2.0

How did your child do when you went and extended your no screen time?

....

....

....

....

How did this week go? Did adding the 30 minutes change anything?

....

....

....

....

What is going well?

....

....

....

....

What was challenging?

....

....

....

....

Did they get emotional without their technology for this long a period?

....

....

....

....

WEEK 9: SCREENTIME & HOMEWORK

ACTIVITY 9: Screen Rule Version 3.0
No screens until homework is complete.

We are going to watch for fireworks here! Your child might even tell you they need the technology for homework. The easiest thing is to remove notifications and put their phone on airplane mode or to limit their use to completing homework only.

Cultivating a Success Mindset is about learning how to be present with what is in front of you. It is about learning how to be present, productive and focused during work time and then present during constructive play and/or family time. This habit will serve your tween or teen as they enter high school, college and eventually the "real world." They need to be able to focus and shut out the distractions. They also need to know when it's time to relax and unwind. Their addiction to screens can be undone just as it was initially done. But, it will take time. It's about retraining the underlying habits.

One of the added benefits of this exercise is that they will also learn they don't have to respond to everything immediately. I have noticed that the Millennials that come to work for me get overwhelmed because they believe that everything must be responded to simultaneously! But, in my office, this is impossible. You can't respond to two requests at the same time or two emails at the same time. I end up having to retrain a lot of bright young people because their sense of urgency is so heightened. By the same token, your child cannot be present with homework and their friends at the same time.

	MON	TUE	WED	THU	FRI
Was your child able to work for the whole homework period without distractions?					
If no, what was the source of the distraction?					
How long did your child predict homework and studying would take today?					
How long did your child actually spend doing homework and studying today?					
Is your child using the designated study space and study time?					

PARENT REFLECTION: SCREEN RULE 3.0

Remember, you may want to extend these times gradually.

How did your child do when you went and extended your screen rule to no screens during homework time?

....

....

....

....

How did this week go? Did eliminating screens create any friction?

....

....

....

....

How much did it impact? Or not?

....

....

....

....

What are some improvements you are seeing?

....

....

....

....

What was challenging?

....

....

....

....

How were you at maintaining your boundary around the study space?

....

....

....

....

How were you at maintaining your boundary around the homework time?

....

....

....

....

How many assignments did they finish?

....

....

....

....

Did they get emotional without their technology for the entire length of their homework?

....

....

....

....

Are you seeing any effect on their relationship to technology generally?

....

....

....

....

Bonus: Screentime & Dinner Time

BONUS ACTIVITY A: SCREEN RULE 4.0
No screens during homework, dinnertime and/or family time.

This activity involves learning how to detach and be present! You might even want to go rogue and decide on no screen time during the entire week. Every parent is different. I like the idea of this exercise because it helps cultivate more time away from the phone.

Bonus: Screen Rule Ideas

BONUS ACTIVITY B: MORE SCREEN RULES

This activity is a bonus for those parents who want some more ideas about other rules and controls to use. There are all sorts of screen rules you can envision!

We raised some of these questions above, but here they are again to further think about:

Do you have blocks and parental controls on internet, social media & television?

....

....

....

....

Do you have any age restrictions on phone or social media usage?

....

....

....

....

Do you have a limited or unlimited data plan?

....

....

....

....

Do you have a rule about being able to see your child's texts?

....

....

....

....

Do you have a rule on what age your child can have an Instagram account?

....

....

....

....

Do you want to create any time limits or weekday/weekend restrictions?

....

....

....

....

5

STICK TO THE
TASK AT HAND

"Success demands singleness of purpose"
-Vince Lombardi

CASE STUDY F
Frank, 9th grade

Frank had come to us with an entirely different set of hurdles. He was underperforming in all of his classes at his new school. While Frank suffered from ADHD, he also had a different issue—he was in major academic distress in most of his classes. My coach went in to determine what was going on. They could only commit to two subjects a week.

Knowing this, the coach went in. Initially we told her she would work on Algebra and History. We have a rule at the company where we need at least a minimum amount of time per class.

However, every time my coach would arrive, instead of being able to tackle history, she was given a different set of priorities. Or, the tutor would start on the history assignment and then mid-way the mother who was listening in, would interrupt and tell them she wanted them to work on a different subject!

Knowing our standard and the work we do, the coach called me in a panic. I told her I would contact the mother.

I did. I let her know that part of the work we do with students that have ADHD is taking a project from start to finish. We don't advise starting multiple projects and leaving them open-ended because that would defeat the mentoring we do with children to show them each step and micro task. The mother, a traditional learner, was perplexed! Why?

The grade on the history paper came back as—incomplete. The teacher pointed out that the child had not completed the assignment as asked. Frank had only turned in what he completed with our coach. She told the coach she was disappointed. Again, we had a follow up consultation with the mother. Children that have learning differences cannot be expected to do things the way we like. They need a longer runway.

She agreed and allowed us to focus on one subject start to finish!

Completing a task and completing it well is an essential skillset for cultivating a Success Mindset. Yet, task completion appears to be a tall task in today's Perfection Age, when tweens, teens and young adults must guard against something more profound—the inability to maintain focus on a single task.[64] We spoke above about the inability of children to properly multi-task but *attention failure* is something deeper. According to Casey Schwartz in the *New York Times*, attention failure is a more recent phenomenon where people of all ages cannot stick to the task at hand because their attention is pulled by their phone or device.[65] In 2016, Apple disclosed that their iPhone customers unlock their phones at least 80 times per day.[66] The deeper concern *should* be that young people today are being conditioned to want to unlock and check their phone or device as much as possible! We all have to be worried when professional baseball players like Red Sox third baseman Pedro Sandoval cannot play through a game without checking Instagram.[67] And, we need to intercede when the Dean of Academic Planning at Columbia laments about how Ivy League students cannot get through the same reading assignments that students 50 years ago could.[68] They are revising academics at one of our most hallowed institutions because kids can't get through the reading—wait, what? It's not only kids with ADD or ADHD, *Attention Failure* is affecting all of us.

Have you noticed that your child has trouble finishing the task in front of them without being distracted? Maybe they keep switching between assignments or between thoughts. They might want to check on the phone you have stashed in the other room. There are a myriad of reasons why a child wants to switch between tasks or assignments: (1) impatience, (2) they are struggling and realize a different task will be easier, (3) something feels more urgent and pressing, (4) they have trouble with task completion because of a diagnosed learning difference, or (5) they are used to having their attention pulled by various notifications and devices.

You cannot discuss task completion without acknowledging that the game has changed so much! We used to think of task completion as a challenge for those kids with a diagnosed learning difference. But, devices and technology have affected everyone's ability to complete tasks—including traditional learners. Whatever the reason—attention failure, learning difference, etc.—you are not helpless to navigate and parent around it.

Learning to Slow Down

I find that kids we work with are increasingly having trouble completing one task at a time—Pedro Sandoval isn't the only one struggling! I have been worried about this for the last few years, but most parents are just now acknowledging the profound influence that devices have had on our attention spans. You need to remind yourself that this crisis may have even been patterned without your knowledge. Your children have been weaned on Netflix, Alexa and iPhones. They answer texts while trying to do homework. Their brains need to unlearn being pulled in twenty directions.

Kids are so over-stimulated that doing one thing at a time seems "basic." Yet, your task will be to do that—to have your child slow down and cultivate their *complete focus* on one thing. We are actually helping them regain their attention. As I tell my coaches, our young student clientele will feel awkward. It might feel "boring." Anyone will feel like they are moving slower until they actually become accustomed to having their complete focus. Just because you, the parent, have taken away their phones during homework time doesn't mean the underlying behavior is not still there. Like a reflex, they will want to switch to something else. When we train teens and tweens to have their complete focus on reading, they speed way up and their accuracy and understanding improve tremendously.

Unlearning Impatience

We have become a culture of wanting everything done now, done perfectly and/or done yesterday. When something takes a child longer than a few minutes to complete or they fail to do something perfectly on first attempt, they get frustrated and want to move to the next task or an entirely different assignment!

Kids think they should operate as quickly as a computer and when they don't, they think something is *wrong* with them. I am going to explore this topic in more depth in chapter 7 but I want to bring this to your attention because I think it's unique to this age. Kids think they have to perform to the level of a computer!

It's something you are going to have to parent through and around. Kids feel so much more pressure to take more AP's and harder classes. College entrance is getting more competitive not because the rates of acceptance have changed, but because there are more marketable applicants applying.[69] The natural response is to want to speed things up and get things done *now*. However, what I am urging you to do is to have them slow down to cultivate their complete focus— at least at first—so that they can actually perform more effectively. You are going to teach them the valuable skill of quality over quantity. What is the point of doing something quickly if it is littered with mistakes? It means more work and that's not as efficient!

"Multitasking" Slows down the Single Task at hand

For so many parents who feel under the gun, the impulse is to do and have your kids do as much as possible as quickly as possible. But, trying to do too much at once or in too little a time span can paralyze the whole process. Many parents call me wanting to see how many things we can cram into one hour. The short answer is not a lot. In fact, we require that middle school parents give us at least 1.5 hours per subject 2 times per week because each task requires a certain amount of time to get completed well. Switching around between tasks or helping a child "get started" on multiple items actually doesn't allow my coaches to get much done in terms of depth. You only end up scratching the surface of an assignment or preparing for a test.

I end up having to turn away a lot of work because it doesn't behoove the child to learn this way. According to the American Psychological Association, "switching" is more detrimental than completing tasks one at a time.[70] Switching around between two or more tasks actually can cost approximately half of someone's productive time.[71]

Fostering Focus

Parents often insist that their child cannot sit for a whole hour to complete tasks. They don't have the self-regulation. Parents also insist that their child simply cannot focus on anything for that long. They try to negotiate a shorter coaching session. My question is always, if we don't address this now, then when? How will they learn how to focus if we don't at least try to help them?

Somewhere in all of our knowledge and awareness about learning differences, there has been a major misunderstanding about the way all kids learn. Just because a child has difficulty focusing doesn't mean they are incapable of learning to focus or even overcoming that difficulty.

The truth is your child can sit still for an hour and more! Have you ever watched them focus on their favorite movie? What about their favorite video game? They have never been compelled to apply that same ability to something they don't like as much.

In any school, progressive or otherwise, classes are at least an hour in length. Many schools have even moved to a block schedule in which classes are up to 90 minutes long.

Kids need to be able to sit and to stick to a single task from start to finish to feel successful. They certainly will need these skills when they move into the real world. Imagine someone who owns a business who cannot sit through a meeting or an actor who cannot complete a table read. It would be fairly unnerving.

Here is the good news—the ability to focus on one task can be learned! It can be nurtured. Just because your child has difficulty today doesn't mean never, it just means not yet! This should definitely be your mantra for our next set of exercises with your child:

Difficulty today doesn't mean never, It just means not yet!

Learning to focus on something we don't like is an important part of skill building. It's about learning the executive functioning skill of self-regulation. This skill is also helpful in learning to delay self-gratification. You might have heard another word for it—patience!

Stanford Marshmallow Test

Many people cite the Stanford Marshmallow test experiment as a predictor for performance.[72] You might have heard about Walter Mischel's groundbreaking experiment asking children to delay eating a marshmallow. In this experiment, the scientists gave children a choice: they could 1) eat the marshmallow placed before them or 2) wait 15 minutes without touching the Marshmallow and get two.

Here is what is important for you as a parent to know. The Stanford Marshmallow experiment tested children's self-control and patience as a determination of overall performance in life. The ability of children to wait the 15 minutes has been linked to overall life success![73] What Mischel argues is that when executive functioning skills like self-regulation and discipline are fostered early on in children, those children perform better on standardized tests and in life in general.[74]

Amendment to the Marshmallow Test

However, there has been an amendment to this finding. Scientists in Rochester have now come to understand that a second factor in the child's life plays a huge role in a child's ability to wait—reliability. The more reliable and stable the child's environment or adult figure, the more likely the child was able to delay gratification.[75] They were able to trust in the person—the adult experimenter—telling them to wait. They were also able to trust that delaying gratification would mean the reward promised. However, for many children, it was an absence of a reliable adult experimenter that affected their decision. What we are now coming to understand is that nurture also plays a huge role in determining whether the child will wait. In other words, if the child knew that the person promising the delayed reward was reliable then they would wait. What does that mean for you? It means consistency is key. The more consistent you can be about your rules, the safer your child will feel with you.

So now what?

Attention failure could be the single most critical issue facing children today. But all is not lost. You can parent through this hurdle. You can teach them to focus and delay gratification—particularly with something they may not want to do. It seems like the *Holy Grail* but it's doable. For our next set of exercises, we are going to practice sticking to one thing at a time—aka sticking to the task at hand. The underlying goal is to help our children learn greater self-control and greater self-compassion.

LET'S GET STARTED:

WEEK 10: TASK COMPLETION

For this week, we are encouraging you to monitor your student's behavior with homework. Are they switchers? Do they have trouble completing routine tasks one at a time? Do they often do two or more activities simultaneously? Do they constantly get up or have difficulty sitting still?

ACTIVITY 10: No changes in any study routine

You are strictly going to monitor their study habits and the time required to complete homework. Here we are going to do more evaluation. With fewer distractions, we can get to unearthing a separate issue--task completion! For younger students, this will be easy because you can oversee homework but for your older children, it will take some communication. You will ask them how many times they switched around to a different assignment either out of boredom, frustration, or lack of focus.

	Monday	Tuesday	Wed	Thursday	Friday
How many times did your child "switch around"?					
Does your child tackle short assignments first? Or does your child start with the "most important" assignment?					
If there was a significant amount of "switching," was it out of boredom, confusion, or habit? Or did they "switch" away from subjects they don't like?					
Is your child using the designated study space and study time?					

PARENT REFLECTION

Most parents don't even think about the benefits of finishing a short task like a worksheet. Completing short tasks can help your child feel a sense of mastery.

How did this week go?

....

....

....

....

What did you observe about their switching?

....

....

....

....

What is continuing to go well? What's working? What was a positive outcome?

....

....

....

....

How are you handling any resistance from your child?

....

....

....

....

How is everything else going? Have you stuck to the study space? The homework times? The screen rules?

....

....

....

....

WEEK 11:

ACTIVITY 11: Take one assignment and complete it without switching or getting up.

Now that your child is adjusting to working without phones, music and notification distractions during homework time, we are going to layer in the additional challenge of sticking to one task at a time without getting up.

For some students, this is not going to be a big deal. As we peel back the layers to their study habits, you might be surprised to see that they have some great instincts. In other students, switching can be a real issue.

But, this is about helping your child learn a different way. It won't always be easy.

I suggest starting with a short homework sheet or creating a list of assignments and looking at the length that each will take. Pick something short that can be completed in one hour, to ensure they do it from start to finish. It will help them feel a sense of mastery.

When your child feels stressed remind them of this mantra:

Difficulty today doesn't mean never,
It just means not yet!

Everything takes practice. They have to keep practicing to get better at putting their attention on something, just like they would keep practicing music or sports.

	MON	TUE	WED	THU	FRI
Was your child able to complete an assignment from start to finish?					
How many times did your child "switch around"?					
If there was a significant amount of "switching," was it out of boredom, confusion, or habit? Or did they "switch" away from subjects they don't like?					
Did sticking to the task at hand help reduce the time spent on homework or did it increase the time spent?					
Is your child using the designated study space and study time?					

WEEK 12:

ACTIVITY 12: Mindfulness Minute

Whether you have a child that is struggling or not, I suggest asking them to take a seated mindfulness break. We are trying to combat the effects of attention failure by building up to more focus and "sit-ability." This will mean breaking through discomfort whether they are a traditional learner or not.

Mindfulness has been shown to help reduce test anxiety and ADHD.[76] I think mindfulness can be helpful for anyone living in today's distracted world. We suggest incorporating a five-minute Mindfulness break every day during homework.

Think of this as a quick Mindfulness (5-)Minute!

Two great mindfulness exercises are:

1. Having your child imagine a favorite memory or experience with their eyes closed as they breathe in and out slowly for five minutes

or

2. Taking a deep breath in as you count to five and then slowly breathing out for five counts. Repeat that rhythmic deep breathing for five minutes.[77]

There are other great meditation techniques that are available on either *ADDitude Magazine* online or UCLA's website.[78]

This is a great tool for you and your child to fall back on when experiencing the desire to switch. When they feel a burning desire to switch or get up, ask them to close their eyes and use the mindfulness technique.

PARENT REFLECTION

Now, take a moment to journal about how this process is going. Parenting tweens and teens is difficult enough without having to become the homework police. The steps in this book are not only an adjustment for your child, they are an adjustment for you as a parent.

Did you attempt the Mindfulness Minute?

....

....

....

....

How was it for you to impose this exercise?

....

....

....

....

How did your child react to this habit?

....

....

....

....

How did this week go?

....

....

....

....

What did you observe about their switching or getting up?

....

....

....

....

WEEK 13:

ACTIVITY 13: Take two or three assignments and complete each without switching.

We are taking an even deeper dive into combatting that desire to switch by building complete focus. Asking children to proceed through multiple assignments that are both long and short will require a buildup of patience. What you are going to do is communicate with your children. You are going to ask how long it took them to complete each assignment in the given time slot. We want to discourage switching. We also want to encourage proper task initiation and task completion.

You may need to inspire your child through positive reinforcement. I suggest getting creative here on how to inspire your child to keep going when the going gets tough.

With younger children, this is about instilling the right behavioral patterns while they are young. You may want to use a sticker chart for the days the child did all of their homework. No sticker for days where the behavior was more difficult.

With older children, this is about self-efficacy. Challenge your student to try to do each assignment without "switching" Remind them of the mantra:

Difficulty today doesn't mean never,
It just means not yet.
They CAN do it.

Remind your child that when they feel the urge to switch and it's not a bathroom break, they should "take five" and incorporate the Mindfulness Minute. If your child has less difficulty, then urge them to "take five" between assignment one and assignment two. When you start to see improvement, you will want to give them praise and positive reinforcement. Children need praise when they do things well and they need consequences when they don't.

	MON	TUE	WED	THU	FRI
Was your child able to complete 2-3 assignments without "switching"?					
How many times did your child "switch around"?					
If there was a significant amount of "switching," was it out of boredom, confusion or habit? Or did they "switch" away from subjects they don't like?					
Did sticking to the task at hand help reduce the time spent on homework or did it increase the time spent?					
Is your child using the designated study space and study time?					
Do you think your child needs an outside accountability partner to help with task completion?					

PARENT REFLECTION

As a reward for all of your hard work, we are going to do a simple reflection exercise. If you haven't already done so, try the mindfulness exercise yourself tonight before bed.

6

FREQUENCY & RECENCY

*"Repetition is the Mother of Learning,
The Father of Action, Which Makes it the Architect
of Accomplishment."*

-Zig Ziglar

CASE STUDY G
Revisiting Caroline, 5th grade

Remember Caroline. Caroline's mother was beside herself. The teachers at school had gently reminded Caroline not to worry about memorizing her times tables. The information would come together over time. Now she was fighting her mom on memorizing times tables.

We decided that we would take a different approach. It's a difficult subject to tread upon. We had to tell the mother that, although we respected the school as a whole, we entirely disagreed with this approach. I told the mother that I, just like she, had learned my times tables by memorizing them. We would experiment with introducing this traditional learning skill of repeating and memorizing information so that we might affect a change in Caroline's ability to do 5th grade math. We would introduce each number like a building block, never leaving a set behind. But, Caroline was going to have to memorize!

By week 10, she had received her first 14/14. As a team, we were elated with her progress.

Do it Again. If you watched the incredible documentary *The Defiant Ones* on HBO in 2017, you would have heard that phrase echoing throughout the show as a common thread.[79] I know because my former assistant Ryann texted me after watching the documentary and said, "You have to watch these guys. They say the same thing you do." Later that weekend I sat and watched this documentary in silence inspired by these two men.

Dr. Dre spent countless hours at his DJ turntables learning about the history of music and sounds. Before that, he spent countless hours learning how to DJ. He put time into learning how to weave together music even in the infancy of his music career. He put time into his craft. Then he found himself digging into learning how to operate an engineering board. When Jimmy Iovine first met Gwen Stefani from No Doubt, he told her she would need 6 more years before she would become a star, but he was certain she would be a star.[80]

Repetition is the key to mastery and confidence. But, most modern teenagers don't realize they have to do something over and over for it to sink in. According to Malcolm Gladwell's book *Outliers*, it takes 10,000 hours to become an expert at any craft.[81] That's roughly 416 days if you did something 24 hours a day. But, what about if you do something 8 hours a day? Well then, it would take you 1250 days to become an expert—roughly 3.5 years. But, that's assuming you do it every single day for 8 hours a day for 3.5 years straight. What if you could only do something for four hours a day—the rough equivalent of a teenager's homework schedule? In this case, it would take you 2500 days to become an expert. This figure brings us closer to about 7 years. And remember, this doesn't account for weekends, holidays, travel, summer camp, etc. In the case of a normal teenager, it would take closer to 8 years to become a true expert at schoolwork.[82]

If you told the modern teenager it would take them 6 years (as in the case of Gwen Stefani) or 7-8 years (like Malcolm Gladwell) to do anything, they would laugh. As I stated earlier, we live in an "insta-culture." In a world where teenagers can order a Lyft in five minutes, get food delivered from Postmates in 30 minutes, and watch anything on demand, time seems like a complete inconvenience. They don't have to wait like we did for a show to come out every week. They don't even have to watch full-length shows. Even the very nature of programming has changed so that kids and teens can consume longer stories in five-minute short episodic bites on their phones on the go.

Invariably, this kind of Jetson's-like instantaneous gratification sets our kids up for a huge fall. They have unrealistic expectations. One hour looking at sheet music, and they think they should be Keith Richards. In fact, they punish themselves for not being Keith Richards. They don't realize that it took Keith Richards years to become Keith Richards.

Repetition: Do it Again

It takes time and repetition to hone skills. Why? Time of course. You can try to escape it, but the truth is that with time and focus any person can become successful. It's about review and repetition. In my philosophy of habit building, I need at least two separate sessions per week to make a dent. Children need both frequency of information and recency.[83] Remember what Dr. Jensen stated about repeating information, "*the connection becomes like a well-worn path through the woods.*"[84]

Frequency and recency is the name of the game. Anyone that has ever worked for me knows that I believe you have to do something over and over again to have it sink into your bones. You have to do it. Over and over. You have to review it in order for a piece of information to move from what is called short-term memory into the longer-term memory.

This has become yet another one of my biggest concerns in the Perfection Age—impatience. I know I keep repeating myself. Parents very often forget that it takes any human three or more times for a piece of information to sink in. Think about how many times you are bombarded with some marketing piece before you decide to act and buy something.

Kids need the same reinforcement. Remember Dr. Jensen from above. Frequency and recency is the name of the game. Tweens and teens can't cram. They need to see something over and over again. As a reminder, you need to tell them something over and over just as I am doing here in this book.

Many parents have come to me with a common misunderstanding about learning in general. A piece of information might sink in on the first or even third exposure. But, skills, habits, and understanding take repeated reinforcement to master. I don't know how many times I have had the following conversation: "great, we would love to sign up but how long is your method going to take to master?"

I hate to give this answer but it's the truth--it takes at least a full year for our students to learn the skills we teach them. It takes a full 18 months to two years to internalize the basics of my Ladder Method.

I also get this persistent problem from parents defecting from other tutoring companies: "My spouse is worried that the coaching isn't working. Our son or daughter spent an hour with the coach on Monday, but we cannot tell if he is gaining ground in his reading skills. The coach has suggested that our son or daughter must read each night to make any headway. We can't pay for tutoring five to six nights a week. And, well we haven't had time to read with our son or daughter. But, we will try. Do you think that might help? What should we do?"

My follow-up comment is always usually something to this effect: "If your child has played a sport, an instrument, or participated in any endeavor outside of school, the teacher, coach, or guide probably has told them they need practice. The same is true for any habit or skill."

We don't like to take on any client who is unwilling to commit. Imagine you have a child practice with a basketball coach 1 hour per week and they practice shooting baskets. You would certainly expect that your child might, without prompting, practice their free-throw 30 min per day either every day or every other day until the next lesson correct? Right. You might also expect that your child would improve slightly over the course of the 7 days, but more so over 30 days, and definitively after 3 months. You would not expect the same results if your child only practiced shooting hoops that one hour each week. You would probably be laughed at if you called a basketball coach after the first one-hour session and asked why your child could not play professionally.

The same is true for reading or exercising or more generally any habit formation. Children need repetition to gain understanding.

CASE STUDY H
Hannah, 1st Grade

This is one of my earliest young students. She was extremely bright, but very young. She was at a strong humanities primary school where they were reading fun early stage books. Anyone who has a first or second grader might be familiar—the Biscuit books. She was just learning her sight words.

We would read and read, but I noticed that Hannah did not have command of her sight words. So we split the session; the first fifteen minutes would be on sight words. The next 30-45 minutes would be on reading the book. I told her we would try to finish the book by the end of the week. She looked at me in complete shock. "What?" she remarked. "I can't do that." I just nodded gently and ignored her. Why not, I thought. If she read with me for 30 minutes each day Monday through Friday, we could certainly finish this book and another one.

The first week was extremely slow. She would get more and more frustrated. Yet, she began to show greater speed at reading. We read daily. With daily practice of her sight words, the words were sticking! This child began to blossom. She wasn't inching her way through these books, she was now breezing through them. The Biscuit book that had taken her one week to complete was now taking her one session to read through. She wasn't just reading for sight words. She was reading for comprehension. I was blown away at her progress.

I knew it was the daily practice.

We made our way through several Biscuit books. Then we moved onto the 100 Dresses book. Then she suggested we try Harry Potter and she was only in first grade.

I noticed several things that would inform my "investigation" into learning. The first was that she got better each day little by little. The second was that she began to anticipate the organization of the lesson. She knew she was going to do vocabulary at the beginning. So, she would spend a little extra time before I got there reviewing so she could show me everything she had learned.

The pieces were coming together for her because there was so much repetition. We didn't lose ground because we had so much time working together. I could see how each building block came together for her. She was mastering reading!

The Return of Performance Anxiety

Performance anxiety has become the de rigueur diagnosis for kids. I constantly hear moms and dads telling my team that their kids are seeing psychologists and psychiatrists because they have incredible performance anxiety. These students tell my staff that they utterly "blank out" when they see the test. My questions always are: *"Were they prepared? Did they study? Do they even know how to study?"*

What we usually find is that the issue lies somewhere in

this mix. The child has not done nearly enough to score an A. It's no wonder they are panicked—they aren't ready!

CASE STUDY I
Isaac, 9th Grade

One of my coaches had come to me with an interesting case. A student of hers, Isaac, was absolutely becoming distraught. He would do wonderfully on his physics homework, but when he got to the tests, he would blank out. I got on the phone with his mother. His mother had explained that Isaac was an anxious child. Isaac's mother surmised that her child was more humanities based. Physics would be a non-event.

She was considering sending Isaac to a psychologist to see if anything could be done about his growing anxiety. I listened quietly. I immediately got off the phone and told my coach to switch the focus on the session to test preparation only.

I wanted to see if Isaac was actually studying sufficiently to pass those tests. Guess what happened. After about two weeks, the coach reported that Isaac's test anxiety went down. He went from getting a D+ on his exams and quizzes to B+s. The acute issue—he wasn't studying sufficiently. He was looking over his outline once or maybe twice. He never bothered to practice any problems or memorize his outline. It was no surprise as to why he felt his mind go blank on the exams. He would panic because he was well aware that he didn't know the information sufficiently.

Isaac was reviewing enough for recognition, but certainly not enough for recall. His performance anxiety was much more a symptom of his misunderstanding of how he should prepare than an actual acute condition.

Students like Isaac end up doing much better when they have a third party sit with them to show them how to study! They actually don't know what studying looks like. These children are best served when they have an accountability partner (tutor or other figure) to walk them through the steps from start to finish. They do need someone making sure the foundation is being laid properly, at least at the outset.

I don't know if I can even count how many kids come to me thinking that after having done something once or twice, they should be expert at it. They don't understand what is what.

There is such a premium put on mastering something overnight. The truth is that no process or skill is mastered overnight. It's a myth. The 21 days thing is not based on scientific data. The 40 day challenges...not helpful either. Science tells us it takes longer than that.

Researcher Phillippa Lally's findings reveal that habits take much longer than 21 or even 40 days![85] According to Lally's 2009 study, the time frame required to build automaticity with a behavior (aka a habit) varied widely but the median was 66 days. It took participants in the study between 18-254 days to build a new habit and many failed to build the habit at all.[86]

Let me say it clearly: a change in your underachiever or over-achiever for that matter <u>cannot happen overnight</u>. Change takes time. It takes small incremental steps. Your child is not going to be a different child after 1 hour of meeting with any coach or me for that matter. It's not going to happen with only 1 hour of coaching a week for even a month. We estimate that it takes a minimum of 2 sessions per week over 12-16 weeks to see growth and 1-1.5 years to see lasting change. This is the perfect time to remind you that:

Change takes time!
My child needs frequency and recency!

They need frequency and recency! I often urge parents as they start with me that the tweens and teens will appear to be going much slower as they learn many of my skills and habits. Invariably, however, the student will speed up as the automaticity of the skill takes hold.

LET'S GET STARTED: BUILDING STUDY HABITS

WEEK 14

ACTIVITY 14: Forming a Good Study Habit

For the next two weeks, our exercise focuses on studying flashcards with your child. Pick a test or quiz that is coming up. Work backward from test day and find time on 3 separate days leading up to the test or quiz that you can study flashcards with your child. Remind yourself:

Change takes time!
My child needs frequency and recency!

A lot of my philosophy on habit formation is about creating the right environment and the right behaviors. But, these next few exercises are about digging into study habits to create the repetition your child needs to learn better!

	Day 1	Day 2	Day 3
Did your child make study materials (like flashcards)?			
Did you and your child study flash-cards together at the scheduled time?			
If no, what got in the way?			
If yes, how did it go? Did you see improvement as your child studied?			

PARENT REFLECTION:

Let's take a moment to journal about how this part of the process is going.

How was it to find three days ahead of a quiz or test to plan out your child's studying?

....

....

....

....

Did you forget? Did you leave it until the last minute? Did you do it?

....

....

....

....

How did they do?

....

....

....

....

What has been the biggest positive outcome?

....

....

....

....

How is the maintenance on other habits going?

....

....

....

....

WEEK 15

ACTIVITY 15: Keep It Up

This week we just keep the good habits going!

	Day 1	Day 2	Day 3
Did your child make study materials (like flashcards)?			
Did you and your child study flash-cards together at the scheduled time?			
If no, what got in the way?			
If yes, how did it go? Did you see improvement as your child studied?			

PARENT REFLECTION

Let's take a moment to journal about how things turned out your second time around.

How was it to find three days for the second test or quiz?

....

....

....

....

Did you forget? Did you do it?

....

....

....

How did they do?

....

....

....

....

7

FACING THE OBSTACLE HEAD ON

"You must do the thing you think you cannot do."

–Eleanor Roosevelt

CASE STUDY J
Jocelyn, 11th grade

Jocelyn had come to us with an entirely different set of hurdles. She was consistently avoiding turning in her assignments. They were stacking up. Jocelyn was on the cusp of getting a D for her third quarter of her junior year. As any second semester junior will tell you, second semester grades are critical. It's any junior's worst nightmare to be in academic distress. Juniors not only have to pass, they need to maintain their grades or even show an upward trajectory!

Jocelyn came to us in just this predicament. I am sure most coaching companies would have turned this child away for fear of not being able to help this otherwise entirely capable human. My office staff all jumped in. My two tutors actually worked for me on certain days of the week in my office, so it was all hands on deck. With permission from the parents, we contacted the teachers and created a comprehensive list of missing assignments. We then determined what she could turn in for partial credit and what was a lost cause. We always call that part "getting the lay of the land." We never go into a house blind, but in this case, there was just so much.

The missing assignments, however, were just the tip of the iceberg. What was a greater issue was that Jocelyn got in the habit of burying her head in the sand. She had a serious case of avoidance. She avoided the assignment, then avoided turning it in when it was late, and then avoided the teacher so as not to "disappoint" the teacher. Her serious case of avoidance was creating a secondary case of major anxiety.

She also had paralysis every time she sat down to write a paper. Imagine my coach's concern when he saw this big list of action items but his new student froze. In fact, Jocelyn became absolutely paralyzed with the idea of approaching her History paper. It's important to note that Jocelyn had also been diagnosed with Executive Functioning issues, so task initiation was a real struggle for her.

The coach patiently sat as she struggled the first day to outline. It took them nearly four hours to get a 4-paragraph essay into an outline form. It was rough. My coach came back to me feeling like they would be able to tackle the writing on Day 2. But, guess what, the child had the same task initiation paralysis that had gotten her off track on Day 1. Instead of pushing her to write anything, he patiently sat until she worked through her emotions and anxieties. They began. One hour in. Instead of getting up or leaving her there, he sat. He wouldn't let her avoid the task. Nor would he let her ignore her fears about the task. After four hours with a learning coach, she was able to sit and write an introduction and first body paragraph. They were scheduled to resume tutoring on Thursday after a day off on Wednesday. He hoped she might take the reins and work on Wednesday, but as you might suspect, she didn't.

There the unfinished paper sat dormant until he returned. She reported being afraid of writing the wrong thing, so she left it until Thursday. That day they were able to make more progress, finishing the entire paper. They turned it in on Friday. Her final grade: B+.

My coach then began to tackle a new essay on Sunday. He remarked that she showed the same difficulty with task initiation. But, he knew how to navigate her personality better and which techniques worked best with her. Progress!

He sat. He waited patiently for her to begin rather than offering her a set of questions to spark thought. She preferred talking out her ideas with him before beginning the outline. More progress! She just didn't like the prodding. She was willing to do some sort of brainstorming. But when they hit the outline, she stopped again. Only this time, he was prepared to sit again until she wanted to start. She did. She began asking him questions. Again, discussion emerged! He sat with her. This session lasted roughly three hours, but a full outline was completed. Grade: B +.

Each day, as they worked on these different papers and short assignments, he was able to help Jocelyn form a writing process. She had never had one. Imagine that. How had she survived those initial years of high school, I wondered. She had never written her essay in stages. She had written everything in stream of consciousness, which basically means she just wrote without thinking through her paragraphs or overall structure. Once she had a plan of attack that she could use on every essay assigned, the avoidance issue began to resolve itself.

Jocelyn proved to us that task avoidance could be "treated" with a simple version of exposure therapy. Just by sitting with Jocelyn while she faced her fears and providing basic study skills, we were able to help those fears melt away and help end the cycle of avoidance that brought her to our door.

It is challenging to rank which of the issues I think is most representative of kids growing up in today's *Perfection Age*, but avoidance is definitely tied for top spot. One of the things I see so often in my office is the little mudslide has turned into a catastrophic avalanche. You know that missing math homework that your child thought was only worth 5 points? Your child neglected to tell you about five other homework assignments which he forgot to turn in. I am talking about 30 points. And, oh by the way, there was also a take home project worth about 30 points of his grade. But, it was Mother's Day, so in the melee your son forgot to tell you the bad news. Unfortunately, that bad news has hit your email inbox. The teacher is upset that your child has ignored her requests to head to after-school math help. Now, the academic dean has sent you an email saying there are only three weeks left of the school year. Your child has a 65 and is in danger of having to go to summer school.

Obstacles avoided often turn from a small landslide into this type of catastrophic avalanche. That's right. What was just one missing assignment somehow magically turns into a big fat zero on a gradebook or a set of zeros on a gradebook.

Or, not memorizing that periodic table now has turned into a persistent inability to pass a chemistry quiz or test.

In our office, we also know that what your child does and doesn't do often helps them build life skills such as resilience and confidence that affect both their school career and their sense of self. School is more than a learning environment. School is a microcosm of life. School is where your child begins to learn how to handle life's challenges and obstacles.

"Each of us must confront our own fears, must come face to face with them. How we handle our fears will determine where we go with the rest of our lives. To experience adventure or to be limited by the fear of it."
-Judy Blume

School is your child's community. It is where your child will potentially first learn how to make a friend, how to write their name, and more importantly how to navigate life's challenges. Yet so many kids that cross my doorstep don't seem to have that resilience that is so crucial to thriving! I believe this lack of resilience stems from a threefold problem.

(1) *Instantaneous Thinking.* Our students are exhibiting a lack of confidence to try new things again, which is ultimately required for any learning process. (2) *Fear of Failure.* There is a lack of understanding about human development. Learning and mistakes are part of life. We need to teach children to view mistakes as part of the learning process. (3) *Over-Nurturing.*

I am sure you have heard of the term helicopter parent. What about a bulldozer parent? You know, the parent who comes into the school to fight their child's battles. No matter what style of parent anyone is, the bottom line: *We are over-nurturing our children*. We are trying too hard to keep them from pain, which teaches them to avoid pain.

Instantaneous Thinking

One misguided belief that I seem to continuously observe in our young teen and tween clientele is the thinking that if it doesn't come fast, it will never come. In other words, if they don't understand math now, they *never* will. Somehow in our Instagram, Instacart, and insta-ready world, insta is everything. It's even buried in our language. Kids are getting culturally conditioned to think that everything should be instant (and on-demand), including their learning. The problem is that their confidence is getting seriously affected. Because when they can't get it, learn it, or understand it in a few moments, they absolutely think there is something wrong with them.

CASE STUDY K
Karim, age 18

I will share another anecdote about a millennial that I recently sat with in a meeting. I was telling Karim about my book and sharing some of the experiences and issues I was observing. He stopped me and said: "Wait, what?" He took a second and then shared with me that he recently had tried water skiing. But, he gave up. After trying to get up one time, and failing to do so as his friends had done, he turned in his skis. Can you imagine? After one attempt, he completely threw in the towel on his water skiing. He told me that he thought it was ridiculous that all of his friends got up but him. In shame, he stopped. He didn't even think to try to do it over and over again. He thought that if he couldn't do it once, it was a foregone conclusion. He could NEVER do it.

The truth is that Karim represents a misperception that seems to be affecting a lot of teens and tweens we work with. This perception problem is pervasive. Can you imagine that? A foregone conclusion. Karim thought if he couldn't get it once, that was it. Done. Over. He's not the only person floating through the doors of my office with that misguided impression. A lot of my students incorrectly think anything and everything should come instantaneously!

By instant, I mean once. If they don't get it once, they will never get it. This also applies to learning. The growing issue, however, is that children don't realize that learning is a process...of steps. Progress is measured in inches. Yet, children are beginning to think of themselves as "incapable" of doing math or theatre or art if they can't get the skills after one or very few tries.

We learned in the last chapter that our culture of "instantaneous-ness" is causing a lot of impatience. They don't think they should or need to spend the time practicing! Not only this, our culture of "insta" is creating a crisis of confidence.

Our kids are incorrectly suffering because they simply don't understand what they don't understand. Learning takes time. There is nothing wrong with them. They are not stupid. They are in fact quite CAPABLE. Our (or rather their) measurement stick is off. We cannot measure their ability to learn against the processing speed of a computer. Learning is measured over time as it builds and grows. The idea that intelligence is something developed over time is the opposite of our insta-culture.[87] More than this, when this faulty assumption is pushed to an extreme, it causes incredible anxiety in our children because they are measuring themselves unfairly. Each child is also unique from other children. Just because their friend might be gifted at math doesn't mean they have the same gift, but it also doesn't mean they are incapable. Different people have different strengths and different weaknesses.

FEAR OF FAILURE

I also have observed a real paralysis in our clientele that stems from fear of failure. They are afraid to be imperfect and make a mistake! But, that fear can create a lot of paralysis. It actually impedes their growth. You might have observed a few offshoots of this in your child: perfectionism, performance anxiety, and low self-esteem.

Perfectionism

Perfectionism is an offshoot of our instantaneous thinking. Perfectionism is the seeking of a perfect standard of behavior and/or results.[88] With perfectionism, the standard is so high; it sets the perfectionist up for continual failure. Relationships, events, and schooling become fraught with pressure and anxiety because it is an endless stream of "contests" to be won or lost. It's no wonder that perfectionists seek so often to avoid the source of stress.

Performance Anxiety

Somewhere along the lines, your child or teenager built up a series of bad experiences with reading, tennis, or insert whatever-activity-they-don't-like. All of a sudden, they identify themselves as incapable. Remember the earlier findings from Dinah Avni-Babad's study on habit formation?

The number one reason why a behavior stops is the incidence of one negative experience.[89] The child may tell you something like "I can't do it" or "I tried but it isn't for me" or "I suck at it." Their evidence lies with one experience or one moment that acts somehow as evidence of their entire perspective on their intelligence. It's faulty thinking.

In more serious settings, children experience blanking out on tests. They begin to identify math or reading as something they are "incapable of." We have had several students shake when looking at a writing assignment or a chemistry lab. Their anxiety became so severe.

Low Self-Esteem

It goes without saying but low self-esteem is a huge part of task avoidance. Students often report fearing the end result or end grade as one of the reasons they avoid the task. Other students report not understanding the assignment given as another reason they avoid the task. Some of our students with ADD/HD or executive functioning often avoid tasks because of their difficulty with task initiation or task completion. It is a layered issue that can compound itself. In other words, the more that a student avoids the task, the greater the consequences (i.e., late penalties, zeros, and incompletes). These punishments only increase the continuing anxiety.

CASE STUDY L
Lincoln, 6th grade

When Lincoln had come to my office, his mother had reported some organizational issues and some task avoidance in English.

One of the initial tasks we undertake with our students is organization. With Lincoln, we started by cleaning out his backpack and noticed hidden papers at the bottom of his bag. It turned out that Lincoln had been hiding his low grades in math (not one of the subjects we were working on). His mother had also found another test with low grades discreetly hidden away from view in his bedroom. He had been avoiding showing his mother these tests in the hopes that she wouldn't find out he had been doing so poorly in his math class.

Unfortunately for Lincoln, his math teacher had emailed home to ask about signed copies of those tests! Ah-ha! The school had a policy that low graded tests had to be signed. Otherwise, Lincoln's mother might never have found out. It turned out Lincoln's fear of judgment and his fear of punishment had led him to squirrel away those tests.

OVER-NURTURING & ENCOURAGED AVOIDANCE

Now we get to the even bigger compound issue-the overbearing helicopter or bulldozer parent. We saw this parenting style go awry in its most extreme form in the 2019 Varsity Blues College Cheating Scandal.

Parents are inadvertently teaching their students to avoid discomfort. A minute before their child is set to fall, they are there to scoop them up. They allow their child to skip the test they aren't ready to take, or they allow their child to play sick when there is a fight at school. The teacher at a ballet class was difficult, so now they're off to find a new ballet class. Forget learning how to handle a difficult or exacting teacher. What happens if the school didn't give their child the classes they wanted, so they send their child to a new school. The teacher wants their child to stay after school to do extra credit, but their child doesn't want to so nothing happens. There are no consequences for the child.

Life is now supposed to be some sort of "pain-free" zone. It is perfectly curated by a well-meaning but over-indulgent parent who thinks by doing all of this they are helping. The problem is they are setting their kids up for an enormously difficult road where their kids now cannot do for themselves!

Reasons for Avoidance

Open up Google and look up task avoidance. It is an actual term of art. At the outset of writing this chapter, task avoidance listed 22,900,000 results. But what is causing all of this self-defeating task avoidant behavior?

Someone in the family is encouraging the avoidance. We have, in a very beautiful way, moved from a culture of strict discipline to parenting that takes a more child-centered approach. It's cultural. Unlike our parents, parents today don't want to apply "strict" discipline. They want to communicate with their children. They genuinely want to do what makes their child happy. But, operating from a place in which a child is told they always need to be happy sends the wrong message. Children cannot always maintain a state of perpetual happiness. Disappointments happen. Discomfort happens. Parents have become afraid to let their children feel that disappointment or hurt. So often, parents will tell me they can't bear to see their child in pain.

Why have we become so afraid to let our children feel uncomfortable?

Here is the issue with continuously telling children to avoid discomfort, they get fearful. They stay stuck. They become afraid to move forward. When they are told it is bad to fall down, they become afraid to take risks and fall. You get the drift. If a child begins to learn that unhappiness is to be avoided at all costs, guess what? They do avoid it. They avoid any feelings of discomfort as well as anyone and anything that creates unpleasantness or discomfort for them. That includes teachers or tests! Remember, one of the most important life skills of a successful human being is resilience.

When I recently read Carol Dweck's article "Carol Dweck Revisits the 'Growth Mindset,'" she acknowledges that parents have overdone it.[90] I shook my hands at the ceiling and said yes! Finally! She feels that parents may have gone a little too far. Dweck is the psychologist who first posited that if you train your student to think positively about their intelligence, they would think positively about themselves.[91] Moreover, if you helped young students of any age realize that their intelligence was something that could be developed, they would see learning and school as a process rather than a finite label.[92] It was a novel concept.

Before Carol Dweck, many parents thought that you could measure intelligence on a basic IQ test. That was that. The result was something that was fixed. Dweck's *Growth Mindset* theory encouraged an entirely different model. Students would be encouraged to think positively about themselves and their intelligence.[93] By thinking positively and by being encouraged to grow their intelligence, they were more likely to do so. Basically, her style focuses on the process.

But, we have "frankensteined" her theory. Parents have incorrectly re-imagined this theory to mean that students have to be insulated from challenge or criticism. For that matter, they should be incorrectly insulated from the truth. They have to be told only positive things. They must be guarded from any personal challenges they face. They must also be protected from any feelings of inadequacy.

The End Product = Avoidance!

We have come to reward effort alone and sometimes no effort at all. I see parents who reward a child for showing up. Dweck argues that we need to reward both effort *and* ingenuity.[94] We need to encourage our children to move beyond trying. Trying is simply not enough. We need to encourage our children to be creative in solving their own problems.[95] We need to encourage them to experiment and not give up at the first sign of trouble.

Children need to be taught that setbacks are also a natural part of the learning process. However, parents today in an attempt to nurture self-esteem have incorrectly rewarded effort alone even when the child gives up at the first sign of challenge. We seem to be incorrectly telling our kids: "it's okay! We don't want you to feel challenged," instead of teaching them that challenge is part of life. The more we can teach that challenges are a part of life and development, the more we can alleviate the stress that comes when they feel even an ounce of discomfort!

But the issue still remains. We seem to have applied the "A for Effort Mindset" incorrectly! So how do we course correct?

PARENT TIME

Like we did above, this is the pause button in the chapter so that we can evaluate our own relationship to our own perfectionism and/or failure.

As a recovering perfectionist myself, I often found myself putting my hands away when I worked with a child because I knew I could do things faster. My impulse back when I started was to jump right in with clients. But I would stop myself because professionally it was counterproductive. So, I understand the impulse. Especially when you see your own child steering in the wrong direction. You want to grab the wheel.

So, let's answer a couple questions about our own relationship to failure:

What is our current relationship to setbacks?

....

....

....

....

PARENTING IN THE AGE of PERFECTION

Have you recently experienced any setbacks at work? At home with your partner? With your extended family?

....

....

....

....

What is your definition of failure? What is the difference between a failure or a mistake?

....

....

....

....

Have you ever experienced social isolation? Bullying? What about social setbacks?

....

....

....

....

Do these answers surprise you?

....

....

....

....

How to Combat Avoidance

Here is the exciting thing. As much as I want you to understand what avoidance is, I don't want you to focus on the negative behavior. We actually counsel our parents not to focus on the negative behavior but rather to focus on forging the good behaviors and positive thinking! It is okay that your child may be actively avoiding his or her source of stress. Remember. It's very human. They are certainly not meant to be perfect. This stage is an opportunity for them to grow and move past this present hurdle.

The way through is always by choosing contrary action—its opposite behavior. So, what is the opposite of avoidance? It's continued engagement with the source of stress. It's... facing the obstacle head on and not giving up. The answer to combatting avoidance and anxiety is to build resilience. You heard me: we need to foster resilience!

Fostering Resilience

The Oxford English dictionary defines "resilience" as "the capacity to recover quickly from difficulties." The second definition of resilience is "the ability of a substance or object to spring back into shape; elasticity."[96] Basically, a resilient person is a person that is able to pick himself or herself back up when they experience difficulty. But I like the second definition as it speaks to a resilient person's ability to be adaptable and flexible!

The more rigid the person or the person's thinking, the more inflexible, unadaptable, and fearful the person is. Flexibility is the key to resilience. Understanding this concept was *mind-blowing* for me. Most people think of resilience as inner toughness, or being like steel. Parents try to make their children immovable and tough, but what resilience speaks to is the student's ability to resume and get back up. This speaks to a person's ability to recover, heal and come back stronger with newfound knowledge and information. It is their ability to keep getting hit by waves and to keep getting back up with deeper understanding about how things work!

Wait....How is it Built?

The truth is that resilience is born from understanding life as a process and teaching our students more mindfulness.[97] Like Carol Dweck has argued, teens and tweens are never "stuck" in a position whether it is academic or social.[98] Life is subject to change.

Discomfort is Okay

We need to remind our children that growth comes from stretching ourselves. One of the first misunderstandings I try to tackle with children and young teenagers is the misperception that life should be entirely comfortable. I try to counsel young kids to understand that doing something they are not good at initially feels awkward. It may even be frustrating! It's new and new is not always easy.

Discomfort = Growth

We also try to tell children that growth can often feel uncomfortable, much like a scab that feels itchy while it's healing! The itch is the signal that your skin is healing. In much the same way, discomfort is a sign that your child is growing.

Understanding Fear:
False Evidence Appearing Real

Another misconception we attempt to correct with children is to understand that fear is not always rooted in truth. My favorite saying is that "FEAR" is "False Evidence Appearing Real". Our children have falsely created a story around their experience or set of experiences that is not necessarily true.

CASE STUDY M
Revisiting Isaac, 9th Grade

Remember our physics student, Isaac? His experience was telling him that he simply was no good at physics. Everything in his mind seemed to add up. But, what if the evidence he had gathered was based on false assumptions? What if his understanding of what it means to "study" was flawed?

I went on to figure out that this was actually the case. My tutor explained that Isaac wasn't spending enough time with the material to actually let it sink in enough. Isaac's evidence, his failed tests and quizzes, seemed to him to mean he could not pass physics. However, his brief reviews of his physics notes were not "studying."

He wasn't studying enough to create "recall" but rather mere "recognition." Of course he was blanking out. He didn't know it well enough to let the information stick. After we "over-prepared" him for his tests, he went in and knew the answers with clarity and certainty! In the end, we were able to help him see the flaw in his thinking. It was False Evidence Appearing Real!

It's okay to make mistakes!

For some reason, our kids are under the incorrect belief that it is not okay to fail or make a mistake. But, mistakes and miscalculations are part of learning. Karim, from the section on Instantaneous Thinking, was a fantastic example of the "worst case thinking." He's the young man from above who had thrown in the towel after one attempt at water-skiing. The underlying problem was in his understanding. His misperception was that he didn't have the traits to be good at water skiing. The correct line of thinking is that water skiing is a sport in which ability can be developed over time. He didn't understand how long something takes to learn, let alone master.

Remember Dweck states that if we teach children that their intelligence can be grown rather than fixed, they think more positively about themselves.[99] I think they have to also understand that part of that path of growth includes failures and miscalculations and discomfort.

I counsel a lot of young teens, tweens and adults that each and every person has a set of gifts, things that come easily, and a set of weaknesses, areas that need strengthening. Humans are not meant to be perfect. We are meant to learn and grow. Our areas of gift come naturally and swiftly. They are usually areas in our life that we take for granted because they come easily. If we are good at math, our homework might only take us thirty minutes. Our "weaknesses," on the other hand, are areas that require more tending and more persistence. Our English essay could take hours or days to work on, at first.

Understanding Failures and Mistakes

We need to help our children understand that mistakes and "failures" are part of life. Let me say that again:

Mistakes are part of life.
Failure is part of life.

Failure is not dispositive. Failure is not evidence that it's over. Failure is merely the beginning. It was something that needed to be learned that has not been integrated yet! We need to teach our children that failure is an important part of development. It actually helps us become stronger.

I like to offer my tweens and teens the example of a scientist. In science, experimentation is a core piece of the subject matter and the experience. Scientists often go into areas where they do not readily even know the answer. They are forced into experimenting with a set of issues until they find an answer. With each experiment, they gather a little more understanding and a little more information that helps with future attempts.

By the same token, I try to explain to people of all ages that life is much like an experiment. With each mistake, you gather a little more intelligence about how to proceed for the next attempt.

Part of building the muscle of resilience is allowing room for it. I remember that many years ago I was trying to raise capital for a startup in 2008. I didn't go to my parents. Instead I went to a family friend who took me under her wing. She was a fabulous mentor. She didn't protect me. She taught me. She pushed me into the lion's den. I knew she understood venture capital and how to raise money. So, I went to get to know her. Instead of giving me advice, she threw me in the deep end of an event in the VC world and introduced me to people. She observed at first. Then, she coached me on how to go up to people. She would model it in front of me. She got in my face. Then she pushed me to do it on my own. Afterwards, she would give me constructive criticism. It was hard to hear at first. She told me my weaknesses and where I could improve. But, she set me on a course for success because she didn't do it for me. She let me fall. And, she was there for me when things went sideways!

Be Brave: Face Your Fears

The final piece of building resilience is facing your fears. The only way to overcome fear is to face the obstacle head on. We are now going to come full circle with your child's avoidance. Has your child ever said, "My teacher hates me! She can't stand me. She treats me different than the other kids. I can't do anything right." Or, some kind of combination thereof?

At my company, I work with all types of kids. We have a great number of students that come to us at the bottom of the class. Believe it or not, those kids all seem to think that their teacher H-A-T-E-S them. At least that is what their parents tell me.

The reality is that it is unlikely that any teacher or authority figure hates any child. But, could it be reasonable to think that a teacher might be frustrated with a child who persistently forgets their homework and then avoids seeking help during office hours? Quite possibly. Teachers are human. They get frustrated when a student isn't working to the best of their abilities. They also recognize when students have a bad attitude. Could the homeroom teacher be concerned about a child who acts out in class? My guess is that it is a very reasonable assumption.

Teachers want their students to succeed. Teachers have seen so much over their careers, both good behavior and bad behavior. They know when kids are not cooperating. They see the signs. In many cases, it is as if they can read the runes. They know when their students are *under*performing. They also know when they are struggling to keep up.

My company prides itself on communicating with teachers. Most of the time, the teachers are spot on. The behavior they observe in class is a mirror image of what I observe in a home session. In my company, I work to try to "root" out the problem by asking a series of questions.

PARENT TIME:

The following questions may be helpful for you to identify where your child may or may not be struggling:

Is your child turning in all of their homework on time?

....

....

....

....

Is your child able to complete the homework?

....

....

....

....

Is your child having trouble keeping up with the pace of the class?

....

....

....

....

If your child had support, could they feasibly keep up?

....

....

....

....

Is your child misbehaving in class?

....

....

....

....

When I begin to work with a family who reports issues with the teacher, the first thing I ask my coaches to do is get the student to turn in the work. Why? Because, it will help quickly turn around the negative feedback loop they are experiencing with their teacher.

What is the Negative Feedback Loop?

In psychology, a "negative feedback loop" is a term used to describe the loop created by a "negative trigger."[100] The loop operates as follows: the student has a bad experience with a teacher. The student then experiences a mental reaction to the experience of being reprimanded by the teacher. The mental reaction creates a negative association with the teacher. The mental reaction may be further exacerbated by negative self-talk. Then finally, the student has a physical reaction to the mental reaction. They might panic, hyperventilate, or get scared. The loop then gets further ingrained because the teacher may continue to reprimand the student about the behavior that is not changing. Students are often unable to understand that the teacher dislikes their *behavior*, not them. This misunderstanding almost always boils down to the student deciding the teacher hates them.

Getting Out of the Negative Feedback Loop

In many ways, I follow a behaviorist's viewpoint: good behavior can be molded through positive reinforcement. It goes without saying that often what is at the crux of the bad behavior is bad reinforcement. The student has taken one of their teacher's reprimands and has become conditioned to expect the worst. After one or two bad experiences with that teacher, they have interpreted the relationship with the teacher as a negative one.

How do you reverse this pattern?

While we cannot undo whatever negative experiences have occurred in the past, we can create new, positive pathways. We create a "positive feedback loop."

Taking Action

We teach teens and tweens that actions speak louder than words. We do this by working with a client to finish current assignments on time. This act of taking responsibility for current work starts the students back on the road to recovery. We actively work on forging a positive relationship with the teacher, who wants to see effort and commitment to their class. When a child doesn't meet their end of the bargain, it can destabilize the whole teacher-student relationship. The only way to stabilize the relationship is to show effort and commitment on the part of your child.

I know I already gave you a short mantra above but before we build on this great new information, I want to share a quote by Nelson Mandela on the importance of working through things with people we don't always like:

"If you want to make peace with your enemy, you have to work with your enemy, then he becomes your friend."
-Nelson Mandela

Although this is not necessarily a mantra, it's something that you need to keep close to you as you begin to ask your child to face people, places and things that are not comfortable for them!

LET'S GET STARTED: FACING FEARS & BUILDING RESILIENCE

WEEK 16

ACTIVITY 16: Self-Advocacy

Find out what your student's lowest grade is currently. Have your student make a list of all missing work or work that got a low grade in that class. Then, have *your* child draft an email from their email address to the teacher. They can copy you, but it must come from them. It must show initiative. The email should express your child's desire to improve and ask about getting partial/late credit on any missing assignments. It should also ask for the teacher's advice and input. Remind your child:

Mistakes are part of life.
Failure is part of life.
Life is like a science experiment, we gather more information for the next attempt!

The goal is not simply to get credit (that is often a matter of class or school policy), but also to start building the skill of self-advocacy. Again, make absolutely sure the email comes from your child (not you!).

Check off when your student has...

__ Made a list of missing work and low grades

__ Emailed the teacher

__ Completed all missing work

__ Turned in all missing work

__ Followed up with the teacher (be sure to express gratitude for the teacher's help!)

Remember to congratulate your child when they follow through. This is essential!

LET'S GET STARTED: BUILDING RESILIENCE

WEEK 17

ACTIVITY 17: Reminding Children of their Long-Term Successes!

In our insta-culture, this can appear to be a tall task. But, it is this task that we have to surmount in order to help our kids learn how to learn.

Our next exercise focuses on getting your child to think about long-term accomplishments. Try to remember an area in which your child has shown great success, despite having difficult moments over a longer period of time. Maybe they are a baseball player and have worked hard to improve their batting score. Or, maybe they are an actor and had to practice their lines over and over to nail an audition.

Building resilience is about reminding your child that not all things come easily. Even those things that come easily require commitment. I have found that in my life, the things I love most still throw me curveballs. It's not only the things we think are our weaknesses.

This exercise is about re-framing and contextualizing how your child views their life. They need to remember when they were successful after having worked hard!

Ask your child a few of the following questions and discuss:

What is a long-term goal that you have worked hard to accomplish? (Maybe it's related to sports, school, boy/girl scouts, etc.)	
How did it feel to accomplish this goal?	
Could you have done it without putting in time and effort?	
What is a long-term goal that you have worked hard to accomplish? (Maybe it's related to sports, school, boy/girl scouts, etc.)	
How did it feel to accomplish this goal?	

WEEK 18

Measuring Success in Inches: Training Children to congratulate themselves after a small victory!

ACTIVITY 18: Ask your child the following questions each day after school.

This exercise is about taking stock of the little victories that your child experiences on the road to success. Remember that great wall you set up earlier in Week 1? This is a reminder to keep using it and congratulate your child on their achievements!

Giving your child positive reinforcement for big or small gains is critical to helping them stay strong on this road.

	MON	TUE	WED	THU	FRI
Was any schoolwork completed today?					
Did you have a positive interaction with a teacher today?					
Did any of your grades improve?					
Did you get any work back today that received full credit or a good grade?					
Did you raise your hand in class to contribute to discussion or ask a question?					
What was one good thing related to school that happened today?					

WEEK 19: CULTIVATING POSITIVE THINKING & GRATITUDE

ACTIVITY 19: Before bedtime, you and your child should list 3-5 good things that happened that day (at least one should be related to academics/school) that they are most grateful for.

As a professed recovering perfectionist, the biggest shift I experienced in my life was the addition of this practice. Being grateful for what is working and where your child is at in life will help them shift to a more positive outlook. It gives them a gentle perspective shift so that they—and you—can keep stock of all the wonderful things they are learning and experiencing. We can take stock more consciously in a practice they can continue. This is the next phase of Activity 18. They can begin to take stock without your gentle questions.

I encourage you and your child to do this together. Do one list for yourself. Your child should do a different list for him or herself. Then read them out loud to each other!

Have fun with this!

Example:

GOOD THINGS LIST / GRATITUDE LIST
1. Got 10 more points on the latest quiz
2. Teacher called on me and I knew the answer!
3. My friends and I had a fun lunch time

Monday

GOOD THINGS LIST / GRATITUDE LIST

Tuesday

GOOD THINGS LIST / GRATITUDE LIST

Wednesday

GOOD THINGS LIST / GRATITUDE LIST

Thursday

GOOD THINGS LIST / GRATITUDE LIST

Friday

GOOD THINGS LIST / GRATITUDE LIST

WEEK 20: CULTIVATING POSITIVE THINKING ABOUT OURSELVES

ACTIVITY 20: Before bedtime, you and your child should list 3-5 good things that happened that day that they are grateful for, and then add 1-2 things that you both like about yourselves.

We do this activity in our Tuesday morning staff meetings and you would be surprised to know that even adults have difficulty identifying those things they like about themselves!

This step of acknowledging your assets is essential to building a healthy sense of self. We all—kids, parents, educators, and others—need a reminder that we have great strengths and great qualities that we need to let shine. It also helps us understand that we are not our "weaknesses." Our day is not only filled with struggle. We need to appreciate our strengths and give thanks for those assets that smooth out our lives!

Again, do this together!

Example:

GRATITUDE LIST	ASSETS LIST
1. Got 10 more points on the latest quiz	**1.** I like that I am the peacemaker of my friend group
2. Teacher called on me and I knew the answer!	**2.** I am a good listener
3. My family	**3.**
4. My friends and I had a fun lunch time	**4.**
5.	**5.**

Monday

GOOD THINGS LIST	ASSETS LIST

Tuesday

GOOD THINGS LIST	ASSETS LIST

Wednesday

GOOD THINGS LIST	ASSETS LIST

Thursday

GOOD THINGS LIST	ASSETS LIST

Friday

GOOD THINGS LIST	ASSETS LIST

PARENT REFLECTION

Take a moment to sit down with your child and discuss how the changes are going.

What is working?

....

....

....

....

What is not working?

....

....

....

....

How do you feel about the changes you are seeing?

....

....

....

....

Are you feeling a shift in your parenting?

....

....

....

....

8

AFTERWORD

"If you are going to achieve excellence in big things, you develop the habit in little matters. Excellence is not an exception, it is a prevailing attitude."

–Colin Powell

Congratulations! You've made it through! I'm so proud of you. You are already making great strides towards giving your child all the right tools to cultivate that Success Mindset.

This journey is *not* about creating the perfect child or forcing your child into any mold. Quite the opposite! I hope we have stripped away all those faulty misperceptions and unfair standards in favor of powerful tools. No person is perfect. We all make mistakes. It's about how we face those fears, failures and uncertainties that will make us happier humans.

My hope is that we, together, can give your child tools so that no matter what the situation, they have a strong foundation. It starts with a nurturing environment, a simple set of routines, improved focus, a little repetition, and above all else a positive sense of self. With the knowledge that they have been able to face small and large obstacles over the last 20 weeks, they will have more faith in themselves! Confidence is built through courage, compassion and love.

You might be thinking: *Oh, no!* Wait. Now what? I finished all of these exercises and I am done?! I myself used to complete self-help books and wonder: *what am I supposed to do now?* I would feel lost. The items in the books had not yet cemented; and I was already cast back out into the darkness!

Let me assure you that you are *not* done. A parent's job is never done. This moment is the next phase of growth. The vision of this book was not to try these habits for 20 weeks and then forget them. I hope that these habits have become part of your child's routine. However, should elements have been more difficult to implement, this book was envisioned as a guidebook to reference continually. You can and should pick it up when you want to re-focus and fine-tune areas. My goal is that you should be seeing a big difference in your child's attitude towards himself or herself.

Rinse and Repeat

I would suggest going through this book one time and then starting over as many times as you need. *Do it again.* See if it becomes easier on the second go around to work through the exercises. What has stuck? What is taking time? What was hard for you? What needs more massaging? I know that in my journey as I repeat steps that I am learning, I go deeper and become more committed as I repeat. I unearth new information as I get better and better. A good set of tools always does that. My hope is that this can be that toolbox for you and your child.

The Ladder Method—the method I developed behind the book—is about building blocks. You might even want to slow down in certain chapters. Maybe you want to repeat the step on homework routines for a few more weeks before moving on to the next chapter. I encourage that. That is always what I have done with my tools. I don't move on with a child until something sticks. This book is yours to tinker with. Maybe you want slow down dramatically with Screen rules and focus before moving forward. Again, this is the corner stone of my method. You don't move forward until an area is *cemented*. With teens and tweens, you need to reinforce skills daily, so everything needs to be carried through weekly as you build skills.

The Myth of the Magic Pill

I also hope that this book has dispelled any common folklore about how transformation and growth work. It can't be attended to for a weekend and then expected to stick without continued application and practice. Remember, we have dumped those faulty Perfection Age thoughts! I want you to have realistic expectations for how change and growth works. I know as a recovering perfectionist myself; I always wanted to get things right on the first try! But, that is often not how life works. I always tell the children in my life that we are all on our own individual timelines! No two lives or life-paths look the same. Thank goodness we get many tries to get things right! Your child needs your support through this process so your positivity coupled with healthy expectations will be key.

Count on Me

Should *you* need support through this process of cultivating a Success Mindset, remember to reach out to your spouse, your friends, a good support group or even me. I am always here to give you a guiding hand should you have questions about what is going right and what may not be! Should you want to get in touch with questions or concerns, please feel free to reach out to me at: **getanswers@theladdermethod.com.** I look forward to hearing from you.

With gratitude.

Candice

Bibliography

[1] Scott, Sam. "Jo Boaler Wants Everyone to Love Math." Wu Tsai Neurosciences Institute. 27 Apr. 2018. 09 June 2019 https://neuroscience.stanford.edu/news/jo-boaler-wants-everyone-love-math.

[2] Wadhera, Mike. "The Information Age Is over; Welcome to the Experience Age – TechCrunch." *TechCrunch*, 10 May 2016, https://techcrunch.com/2016/05/09/the-information-age-is-over-welcome-to-the-experience-age/

[3] Wadhera, Mike. "The Information Age Is over; Welcome to the Experience Age – TechCrunch." *TechCrunch*, 10 May 2016, https://techcrunch.com/2016/05/09/the-information-age-is-over-welcome-to-the-experience-age/

[4] Wadhera, Mike. "The Information Age Is over; Welcome to the Experience Age – TechCrunch." *TechCrunch*, 10 May 2016, https://techcrunch.com/2016/05/09/the-information-age-is-over-welcome-to-the-experience-age

[5] Jensen, Frances E. and Nutt, Amy Ellis. "Building a Brain." *The Teenage Brain: A Neuroscientist's Survival Guide to Raising Adolescents and Young Adults*. 2016, pp. at 37.

[6] Ibid. at pp. at 37.

[7] Ibid. at pp. at 26.

[8] Ibid. at pp. at 79. Arthur Jensen. "How Much Can We Boost IQ and Scholastic Achievement." *Harvard Educational Review*, vol. 39, no. 1, pp. 1-123. 1969.

[9] Ibid. pp. at 37-38.

[10] Ibid. at pp. at 18, 23, 33.

[11] Chödrön Pema. *Start Where You Are: A Guide to Compassionate Living*. Shambhala, 2018.

[12] Author unknown. Many people attribute this phrase to Alcoholics Anonymous and 12 step recovery.

[13] "State-Dependent Learning." *Dictionary.com*, www.dictionary.com/browse/state-dependent-learning. Schramke, CJ.

"State dependent learning in older and younger adults." Bauer, R.M. *Psychology Aging,* vol. 12, no. 2, 1997. pp. 255 – 262 at 255. *PsychNet,* https://psycnet.apa.org/978ada4e-19cb-4e94-b792-73a850a48669.

[14] Godden, D. R., & Baddeley, A. D. "Context-dependent memory in two natural environments: On land and underwater." *British Journal of Psychology, vol. 66,* no. 3, 1975, pp. 325-331.

[15] Schramke, CJ. "State dependent learning in older and younger adults." Bauer, R.M. *Psychology Aging,* vol. 12, no. 2, 1997. pp. 255 – 262 at 257. *PsychNet,*https://psycnet.apa.org/978ada4e-19cb-4e94-b792-73a850a48669.

[16] Perham, Nick. "Can Preference for Background Music Mediate the Irrelevant Sound Effect?" Joanne Vizard. *Applied Cognitive Psychology,* vol. 25, no. 4, 2010, pp. 625-631. Wiley. onlinelibrary.wiley.com/doi/epdf/10.1002/acp.1731?r3_referer=wol.

[17] Jensen, Frances E. and Nutt, Amy Ellis. "Introduction." *The Teenage Brain: A Neuroscientist's Survival Guide to Raising Adolescents and Young Adults.* 2016, pp. at 9.

Guppenberger, David. "State-Dependent Learning and False Memory." St. Bonaventure University. Unpublished dissertation.

[18] Jensen, Frances E. and Nutt, Amy Ellis. "Introduction." *The Teenage Brain: A Neuroscientist's Survival Guide to Raising Adolescents and Young Adults.* 2016. pp. at 9.

[19] "Routine." Def. 1. *Oxford Dictionaries.com,* Oxford Dictionaries, (n.d.). https://en.oxforddictionaries.com/definition/routine

[20] Avni-Babad, Dinah. "Routine and Feelings of Safety, Confidence, and Well-Being." *British Journal of Psychology,* vol. 102, no. 2, 2011, pp. 223–244. *Wiley.* https://onlinelibrary.wiley.com/doi/abs/10.1348/000712610X513617.

[21] Ibid.

[22] Ibid. pp at 226.

[23] Avni-Babad, Dinah. "Routine and Feelings of Safety,

Confidence, and Well-Being." *British Journal of Psychology*, vol. 102, no. 2, 2011, pp. 223–244 at 246. *Wiley*. https://onlinelibrary. wiley.com/doi/abs/10.1348/000712610X513617.

[24] Ibid. pp at 226.

[25] Ibid.

[26] Zajonc, R.B. "Mere Exposure: A Gateway to the Subliminal." *Current Directions in Psychological Science*, vol. 10, no. 6, 2001, pp. 224 – 228 at 225.

[27] Ibid. pp. at 226.

[28] Ibid.

[29] Jensen, Frances E. and Nutt, Amy Ellis. "Building a Brain." *The Teenage Brain: A Neuroscientist's Survival Guide to Raising Adolescents and Young Adults*. 2016, pp. at 33.

[30] Ibid. pp at 73.

[31] Ibid.

[32] Currey, Mason. *Daily Rituals: How Artists Work*. Alfred A. Knopf, 2016.

[33] Currey, Mason. "Pablo Picasso." *Daily Rituals: How Artists Work*, Alfred A. Knopf, 2016, pp. at 94 – 96.

[34] Ibid.

[35] Currey, Mason. "Earnest Hemingway." *Daily Rituals: How Artists Work*, Alfred A. Knopf, 2016, pp. at 51-52

[36] Ibid. pp. at 53.

[37] Currey, Mason. "Albert Einstein." *Daily Rituals: How Artists Work*, Alfred A. Knopf, 2016, pp. at 196 – 197.

[38] Currey, Mason. "Twyla Tharp." *Daily Rituals: How Artists Work*, Alfred A. Knopf, 2016, pp. at 222–223.

[39] Currey, Mason. "Maya Angelou." *Daily Rituals: How Artists Work*. Alfred A. Knopf, 2016, pp. at 122-123.

[40] Ibid. pp. at 122-123.

[41] Kirschner, Paul A., and Aryn C. Karpinski. "Facebook® and academic performance." *Computers in Human Behavior*, vol. 26, no. 6, (2010), 1237-1245 at 1238.

[42] Bilton, Nick. "Either You F—k Me, or I'll F—k You: How Zuckerberg's Billionaires Club Can Atone for Facebook." *The*

Hive, Vanity Fair, 27 May 2019, https://www.vanityfair.com/news/2019/05/how-zuckerbergs-billionaires-club-can-atone-for-facebook.

[43] Ibid.

[44] Ibid.

[45] Perham, Nick. "Can Preference for Background Music Mediate the Irrelevant Sound Effect?" Joanne Vizard. *Applied Cognitive Psychology*, vol. 25, no. 4, 2010, pp. 625-631. Wiley.

[46] Weller, Chris. "Bill Gates and Steve Jobs Raised Their Kids Tech-Free - and It Should've Been a Red Flag." *The Independent*, 27 Oct. 2017, *Independent Digital News and Media*, https://www.independent.co.uk/life-style/gadgets-and-tech/bill-gates-and-steve-jobs-raised-their-kids-techfree-and-it-shouldve-been-a-red-flag-a8017136.html.

[47] Bilton, Nick. "Steve Jobs Was a Low-Tech Parent." *The New York Times*, 10 Sept. 2014, *Newspaper Source*. https://www.nytimes.com/2014/09/11/fashion/steve-jobs-apple-was-a-low-tech-parent.html.

[48] Ibid.

[49] Ibid.

[50] Ibid.

[51] Ibid.

[52] Ibid.

[53] Xu, LingBei. (2008) "Impact of simultaneous collaborative multi-tasking on communication performance and experience." Unpublished Dissertation. Ohio State University.

[54] Jensen, Frances E. and Nutt, Amy Ellis. "Building a Brain." *The Teenage Brain: A Neuroscientist's Survival Guide to Raising Adolescents and Young Adults.* 2016. pp. at 41-42.

Kirschner, Paul A., et al. "Facebook® and academic performance." *Computers in Human Behavior*, vol. 26, no. 6, 2010, pp at 1237-1245, at 1238.

[55] Kirschner, Paul A., et al. "Facebook® and academic performance." *Computers in Human Behavior*, vol. 26, no. 6, 2010, pp at 1237-1245.

[56] Ibid.

[57] Ibid pp at 1238.

[58] "Distracted Driving | Motor Vehicle Safety | CDC Injury Center." *Centers for Disease Control and Prevention*, Centers for Disease Control and Prevention, https://www.cdc.gov/motorvehiclesafety/distracted_driving/index.html

"U Drive. U Text. U Pay." *NHTSA*, 8 May 2019, https://www.nhtsa.gov/campaign/distracted-driving.

Kirschner, Paul A., et al. "Facebook® and academic performance." *Computers in Human Behavior*, vol. 26, no. 6, 2010, pp at 1237-1245 at 1239.

[59] Austin, Michael. "Texting While Driving: How Dangerous Is It?" *Car and Driver*, 24 June 2009, https://www.caranddriver.com/features/a16580948/texting-while-driving-how-dangerous-is-it/

[60] "Austin, Michael. "Texting While Driving: How Dangerous Is It?" *Car and Driver*, 27 Mar. 2019, www.caranddriver.com/features/a16580948/texting-while-driving-how-dangerous-is-it/.

[61] Xu, LingBei. (2008) "Impact of simultaneous collaborative multi-tasking on communication performance and experience." Unpublished Dissertation. Ohio State University.

Guppenberger, David. "State-Dependent Learning and False Memory." Unpublished Dissertation. St. Bonaventure University.

[62] Xu, LingBei. (2008) "Impact of simultaneous collaborative multi-tasking on communication performance and experience." Unpublished Dissertation. Ohio State University, pp. at 79-80.

[63] Xu, LingBei. (2008) "Impact of simultaneous collaborative multi-tasking on communication performance and experience." Unpublished Dissertation. Ohio State University.

Guppenberger, David. "State-Dependent Learning and False Memory." Unpublished Dissertation. St. Bonaventure University.

[64] Schwartz, Casey. "Finding It Hard to Focus? Maybe It's Not Your Fault." *The New York Times*, 14 Aug. 2018, *Newspaper Source*. https://www.nytimes.com/2018/08/14/style/how-can-i-focus-better.html.

[65] Schwartz, Casey. "Finding It Hard to Focus? Maybe It's Not Your Fault." *The New York Times*, 14 Aug. 2018, *Newspaper Source*. www.nytimes.com/2018/08/14/style/how-can-i-focus-better.html.

[66] Statt, Nick. "Apple Says the Average iPhone Is Unlocked 80 Times a Day." *The Verge*, 18 Apr. 2016, *Magazine Source*. https://www.theverge.com/2016/4/18/11454976/apple-iphone-use-data-unlock-stats.

[67] Schwartz, Casey. "Finding It Hard to Focus? Maybe It's Not Your Fault." *The New York Times*, 14 Aug. 2018, *Newspaper Source*. https://www.nytimes.com/2018/08/14/style/how-can-i-focus-better.html.

[68] Ibid.

[69] Urist, Jacoba. "Is College Really Harder to Get Into Than It Used To Be?" *The Atlantic*, Atlantic Media Company, 4 Apr. 2014, *Popular Magazines*. https://www.theatlantic.com/education/archive/2014/04/is-college-really-harder-to-get-into-than-it-used-to-be/360114/.

[70] "Multitasking: Switching Costs." *American Psychological Association*, American Psychological Association, https://www.apa.org/research/action/multitask

[71] Ibid.

[72] Mischel, Walter. *The Marshmallow Test: Why Self-Control is the Engine of Success*. Little Brown & Company, 2014.

[73] Ibid. pp at 106-109.

[74] Ibid.

[75] Kidd, Celeste, et al. "Rational Snacking: Young Children's Decision-Making on the Marshmallow Task Is Moderated by Beliefs about Environmental Reliability." *Cognition*, vol. 126, no.1, 2013, pp. 109-114, pp at 112-113. *Science Direct*. https://www.sciencedirect.com/science/article/pii/S0010027712001849?via%3Dihub

[76] Sherman, Carl. "Mindful Awareness: How to Combat ADHD Symptoms with Meditation." *ADDitude*, ADDitude Magazine, 9 May 2019, https://www.additudemag.com/mindfulness-meditation-for-adhd

⁷⁷ Sherman, Carl. "Mindful Meditation: ADHS Symptom Relief with Breath." ADDitude, ADDitude Magazine, 9 May 2019, https://www.additudemag.com/mindfulness-meditation-for-adhd/

⁷⁸ Ibid.

⁷⁹ Hughes, Allen, et al. Season 1, The Defiant Ones, episode Part One, HBO, 2017.

⁸⁰ Ibid.

⁸¹ Gladwell, Malcolm. "The 10,000 Hour Rule: In Hamburg, We had to Play for Eight Hours." *Outliers: The Story of Success.* Little Brown & Company, 2012 at 39.

⁸² Ibid.

⁸³ Jensen, Frances E. and Nutt, Amy Ellis. "Learning: The Job of the Teenage Brain." *The Teenage Brain: A Neuroscientist's Survival Guide to Raising Adolescents and Young Adults.* 2016, pp. at 73.

⁸⁴ Ibid.

⁸⁵ Lally, Phillippa, et al. "How Are Habits Formed: Modeling Habit Formation in the Real World." *European Journal of Social Psychology*, vol. 40, no. 6, 2009, pp. 998–1009, pp. at 1002. doi:10.1002/ejsp.674.

⁸⁶ Ibid.

⁸⁷ Yeager, David et al. "Mindsets that promote resilience: When students believe that personal characteristics can be developed." *Educational Psychologist*, vol. 47, no. 10, 2012. pp. 302-314, pp at 303. doi:10.1080/00461520.2012.722805.

⁸⁸ "Perfectionist." Def. 1. *Oxford Dictionaries.com*, Oxford Dictionaries, (n.d.).

⁸⁹ Avni-Babad, Dinah. "Routine and Feelings of Safety, Confidence, and Well-Being." *British Journal of Psychology*, vol. 102, no. 2, 2011, pp. 223–244 at 226. https://onlinelibrary.wiley.com/doi/abs/10.1348/000712610X513617

⁹⁰ Dweck, Carol. "Carol Dweck Revisits the 'Growth Mindset.' *Education Week*, September 2015. https://www.edweek.org/ew/articles/2015/09/23/carol-dweck-revisits-the-growth-mindset.html

[91] Yeager, David et al. "Mindsets that promote resilience: When students believe that personal characteristics can be developed." *Educational Psychologist*, vol. 47, no. 10, 2012. pp. 302-314, pp at 303. doi:10.1080/00461520.2012.722805.

[92] Ibid.

[93] Ibid.

[94] Dweck, Carol. "Carol Dweck Revisits the 'Growth Mindset.' *Education Week*, September 2015. https://www.edweek.org/ew/articles/2015/09/23/carol-dweck-revisits-the-growth-mindset.html.

[95] Ibid.

[96] "Resilience." Def. 1. *Oxford Dictionaries.com*, Oxford Dictionaries, (n.d.)."Resilience." *Merriam-Webster.com*. Merriam-Webster. (n.d.)

[97] Yeager, David et al. "Mindsets that promote resilience: When students believe that personal characteristics can be developed." *Educational Psychologist*, vol. 47, no. 10, 2012. pp. 302-314, pp at 303. doi:10.1080/00461520.2012.722805.

[98] Ibid.

[99] Ibid.

[100] "Negative feedback loop." Definition. Patel, Ranjan. "Addressing Anxiety and the Negative Feedback Loop." *GoodTherapy.org Therapy Blog*, 10 July 2014, www.goodtherapy.org/blog/addressing-anxiety-and-the-negative-feedback-loop-0124137

Boskey, Elizabeth. "How Negative Feedback Loops Work in the Body." *Verywell Health*, Verywell Health, 30 Apr. 2019 https;//www.verywellhealth.com/what-is-a-negative-feedback-loop-313287

Made in the USA
Middletown, DE
07 April 2021